The No-Nonsense Guide to Heat Wave, Drought, & Hot Weather Safety

Jeffery D. Sims

Books may be purchased by contacting the publisher and author at Lulu.com, Amazon.com, or contact the author at:

Beyond The Spectrum Books
http://beyond-the-political-spectrum.blogspot.com/

Cover Design: Jeffery D. Sims
Publisher: Lulu Books & Beyond The Spectrum Books
ISBN: 978-1-312-68326-6
1. Reference 2. Science 3. Weather 4. Safety 5. Hot Weather. 6. Heat Waves 7. Droughts
First Edition
Printed in North Carolina, USA

Acknowledgement

The following is a list of the people I'd like to thank for believing in me and my dreams:

... (no, I didn't skip anyone).

Table of Contents

The No-Nonsense Guice To Heat Wave, Drought, & Hot Weather Safety

Introduction

Simply put, in some ways I was a normal child while in other ways I was anything but. It is the abnormal part of my being which accounts for why you are holding this book in your hot little hands (or reading it on your tablet). While I enjoyed watching cartoons, reading comic books, and favored science-fiction (notice a pattern?), I was also fascinated—infatuated actually—with learning about strange, unusual, and otherwise unexplained uncommon events. Whether the subject was verifying the legitimacy of alleged occurrences explored in the field of parapsychology, learning about what things exist beyond the boundaries of our planet through the area of astronomy, or—of relevance to you the reader—understanding the causes of interesting weather phenomenon like tornadoes and hurricanes.

As an adult, my love of learning had grown to encompass many other subjects, including history and politics (which I went to college to study). I had come to the awareness that I had/have an innate thirst for knowledge, about everything around me. As a result, I have more books than I will ever read, probably more than the average person. I've also probably had more different types of jobs than the average person. I've done a great deal of living. And in everything I've read, done, and observed, I've taken a great deal of awareness about life and the nature of the universe around us with me (yes, I know...a little grandiose, if not self-centered-sounding). I suppose by way of osmosis, I had also developed a love of teaching after having fallen into the vocation of substitute and adult education instructor. Because of these experiences, I have been driven to observe the world with an attempt to gain a deeper meaning of it all...and maybe bring a little bit of insight to others.

I am also driven to write about my observations –without the latent bias of emotion, beliefs, or cultural beliefs—in order to convey a semblance of truth (the "teacher" in me I suppose) and maybe give others a little something to think about. This is why I started blogging and writing regularly some years ago. In an indirect way, writing is also a way for me to help others to think about and offer possible solutions to grander problems posed by counterproductive policies and our own individual thinking. But it was only recently that I was motivated to combine my proclivity for (objective) observation, thirst for learning, and ultimately my writing to create a series of books based on my own intellectual curiosities and love for seeking solutions to existing problems.

This resulting compendium of interests and ideas has the (intended) benefit of imparting in those who chose to purchase and read it a level of awareness and knowledge about the an aspect of the dangers –those presented by the earth we live on—inherent in the world around us. And although there are no certain safe places to hide from real-life dangers, there *are* places as well as courses of actions that one can take to limit exposure to these dangers. I acknowledge this fact throughout the book(s) by using terms like *relatively*, *comparatively*, or variations of such words to convey that the suggestions offered are in, all likelihood based on research and other findings, the best options given the dangers and circumstances.

It is my hope that the information in this book (or as I call it, "safety manual") will save a life, or at least prevent serious injury to those who would might be affected by a related dangerous experience.

So without further ado, I present to you, The No-Nonsense Guide to Heat Wave, Drought, & Hot Weather Safety...
--Jeffery D. Sims

Heat Waves
What Are They?

Around the world every summer, different geographic regions experience a fluctuating range of warmer temperatures due to naturally-shifting weather patterns. But occasionally, these changing weather patterns can become stagnant, resulting in repetitive phases of steady high temperatures with very little precipitation (rain). In some cases, the result is a *heat wave*.

In the world of general weather forecasting, heat waves are simply defined as an extended period of unusually hot weather. This is particularly the true for regions that undergo seasonal transitions between warmer and cooler weather patterns. And though heat waves are characterized by several meteorological components, it is the presence of stubbornly <u>unseasonable warmth</u> that signifies to most that a heat wave is underway.

Heat waves are generally defined by their periods of uncomfortably hot temperatures of at least 10 degrees Fahrenheit (5-degrees Celsius) more than the average temperature for a particular geographical region.[1] Daytime temperatures during a heat wave tend to create stifling conditions, with very little relief coming during the "cooler" evening and nighttime hours. And while temperature variations entailing higher than average temperatures can and do occur in cooler months, true heat waves happen exclusively during the warmer weather months (late spring to early fall) due to the warming of the air to uncomfortable and dangerous levels. Weather forecasters may, for example, call a period of 60-degree weather in early December a "heat wave," such an application is normally done so facetiously, and is— or should be—generally understood that such an occurrences not considered a true heat wave.

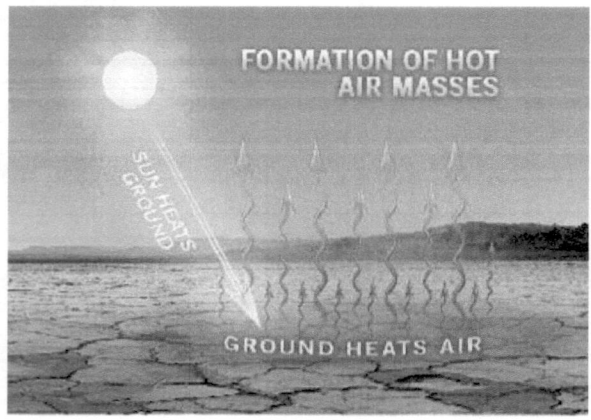

---

[1] Temperature differences as compared to the average mean temperature for said region during the same time of year.

Stationary high pressure air masses are another distinguishing feature of a heat wave. As with most meteorological events, heat waves are the result of interactions between areas of high and low air pressure, moved along by the various jet streams[2] high up in the atmosphere. Atmospheric pressure pull airs to the ground from the upper levels of the atmosphere, creating what's known as a *high pressure air mass.*[3] This action compresses and keeps the air near mass close to the Earth's surface, which also increases its temperature. This action tends to hamper upward air flow, which limits the formation of both any potentially cooling winds at the surface as well as clouds. The lack of clouds and appreciable winds prevents rain and cooler temperatures from occurring. The resulting warm air mass becomes stationary over a particular geographical area, resulting in extended periods of high temperatures over the affected region.

A map illustrating the formation of a heat wave over the continental United States below retreating jet stream winds.

Heat waves are often accompanied by levels *of* high humidity. Humidity, the measure of how much moisture is in the air, tends to impact the effect that hot weather has on the human body. The amount of humidity, when combined with high temperatures, will yield an approximation of *relative humidity*— the amount of moisture the air can hold in relation to present temperatures. A reading of high relative humidity is a measure of how uncomfortable the air feels to those of us experiencing a particular combination of humidity and high temperatures. As an example, if the relative humidity is estimated to be 50%, then the air is half-saturated with moisture. And the higher the relative humidity (combined with higher temperatures), the more uncomfortable we feel. If the moisture content of the air indicates a level of 100% relative humidity, the human body will not be able to cool itself by the evaporation of sweat into the air because the air is already saturated to its limit with moisture. The effect of high

---

[2] Jet streams are the river of strong air currents that flow high in the atmosphere which influence the Earth's climatic patterns. In many cases, these high winds also move weather systems across the atmosphere, while being typically confined within certain longitudes (see page 10 for an illustration of how these wind currents affect the earth's weather patterns).

[3] A high pressure system, or "high," is an area where the atmospheric pressure is greater than that of the surrounding area. High pressure areas (or "systems") result when the air within the high cools and becomes denser and moves toward the ground. The pressure then increases at this point because more air fills the space left from previous lower pressure in the region over which this takes place. High pressure regions are characterized by an absence of clouds, rain, and (usually) winds.

relative humidity then is that we will often feel much hotter than the actual temperature indicates. This relative effect on the human body of high temperatures, combined with high relative humidity levels is called the "heat index" (see the section under "What Makes Them Dangerous?").

Finally, in addition to unseasonably warm temperatures, stagnant high-pressure air masses, and high relative humidity, a heat wave is characterized by its duration. But while many a layperson might understand that heat waves are periods of prolonged high temperatures occurring over a span of time, the actual definition varies from region to region across the globe. For example, the World Meteorological Organization[4] defines a heat wave as a period of time when the daily maximum temperature of more than 5 consecutive days exceeds the average maximum temperature by 9 degrees F (5 °C). But since the average maximum temperature of one region might be different than another region, the point where consistently high temperatures—and related conditions—are recognized to an actual heat wave will vary among regions. In the Netherlands, a region known for moderate weather, an official heat wave has a relatively low temperature threshold, defined as period of at least 5 consecutive days in which the maximum temperature in exceeds 77 °F (25°C)...provided that on at least 3 days within this period, the maximum temperature exceeds 86 °F (30 °C). This particular definition of a heat wave also applies to several other European countries. But in regions in South Australia, a heat wave is defined as 5 consecutive days at or above 95 °F (35°C), or 3 consecutive days at or over 104 °F (40°C). Even in the U.S., the definition (and recognition) of an official heat wave can vary from region to region. While many areas consider a heat wave to be a period of high temperatures for a period of 2 of more days, many areas of the Northeast define a heat wave as 3 or more days at 90 °F (32.2°C). In other areas of the U.S. (as well as other English-speaking regions of the world), these recognitions are dependent upon the accompanying criteria of the heat index.

As with the differences in temperature thresholds among different heat waves, heat waves themselves are not all the same. While many that occur in regions with seasonal transitions regularly contain high levels of relative humidity, those that happen in drier climates may not—and vice-versa. What's more, some heat waves may last for several days, while others might last for a week or more. And heat wave temperatures will usually be much hotter in a region that regularly experiences hot temperatures than they are in regions which are usually cooler overall. This means that temperatures during a heat wave in southern California, where summers are usually hot, may climb to 100-130°F (38-54°C), while temperatures during a heat wave in London, England, where summers are usually mild, may only be 90-95°F (32-35°C).

Whatever the particular threshold, the most relevant aspect of this potential weather emergency is the duration of unhealthy levels of high temperatures and humidity. The longer such conditions persist in any affected region, the greater the likelihood for heat-related health issues affecting those living in such areas. In extreme cases of particularly lengthy intense heat (and limited precipitation), heat waves can become just as devastating *droughts*.

---

[4] The World Meteorological Organization (WMO) is a specialized agency that operates under the United Nations (UN), and overseas research related to meteorology (weather and climate), operational hydrology (water) and other related geophysical sciences such as oceanography and atmospheric chemistry.

Droughts
What Are They?

In the most general sense, a drought is the prolonged deficiency of precipitation (rain) over an extended period of time. And like heat waves, droughts are the result of normally shifting weather patterns creating phases of repetitively dry (and at times, hot) weather. However, unlike heat waves, droughts can—instead of days—last anywhere from several weeks to a season or more—even years.

And recognizing and identifying droughts is not as clear-cut a procedure as recognizing a heat wave. This is due to the difficulties in quantifying how individual droughts vary in their duration, intensity, and impact over an affected area. In most cases, the occurrence of drought is usually not evident until one is underway...usually indicated by sinking water and/or precipitation levels. This means that meteorological recognition of drought conditions is dependent upon how changes in certain environmental factors impact the affected region. These environmental factors include the previously noted absence of precipitation/rainfall, the lower water levels of affected waterways such as rivers and reservoirs, the average temperature within the affected region, the moisture content within local soil within the affected region, and effects on local agriculture (i.e., crops). For this reason, droughts are mostly categorized by 3 main drought types:

1. Hydrological Drought-During this type of drought, waterways such as rivers, lakes, and reservoirs experience depleted amounts of available water.
2. Agricultural Drought- When the lack of moisture level within the soil begins to adversely affect local crops, the agricultural industry will identify an agricultural drought. Shortages in precipitation and reduced ground water levels can also create stress and problems for crops.
3. Meteorological Drought- A meteorological drought is characterized by severely limited and/or absent precipitation. This is to say that an area that normally receives less rain than usual can be considered in a drought. This is also the most common type of drought, as it tends to affect water levels of local waterways as well as other aspects on an affected region's economic infrastructure (such as agriculture). Additionally, most locations in other parts of the world have their own meteorological definition of drought, based on the climate norms in their respective areas.

Since changes in several environmental variables need to be considered for a region to be designated drought-stricken, it is very difficult to determine when in particular a drought begins (again, some time may pass before a drought is known to even be occurring). As a result, this makes defining a drought somewhat relative—dependent upon what aspect of a region's environment is [negatively] impacted. To a farmer, a drought might be a prolonged stretch of time without rainfall that affects the crops under cultivation; even 2 weeks without rainfall can stress many crops during certain periods of the growing cycle. To a water manager or hydrologist, a drought is a deficiency in water supply that negatively affects the availability and water quality. This might mean the point in time when river and reservoir levels become alarmingly low. And to a meteorologist, a drought is a prolonged period when precipitation is less than normal, causing concern such as increased fire dangers (see the section, "Why

Are They Dangerous?"). For these reasons, it is only *generally* understood that a drought is an extended period when a region experiences a deficit in its water supply, whether atmospheric, surface or ground water. It is only in the most extreme cases of water/precipitation deficits that it is generally accepted that a drought is underway.

The most well-known historical case of this instance was the period in American history known as the "The Dust Bowl" period. *The Dust Bowl* was the name given to the part of America's Great Plains region that experienced a particularly devastating drought during the decade of the 1930's. A 150,000-square-mile (388.60 square km) area encompassing parts of Oklahoma, Texas, Kansas, Colorado, and New Mexico, was affected by a combination of conditions that included scarce rainfall, prolonged high temperatures, high winds, and loose soil brought on by drought and poor farming practices. The combination of these factors ultimately depleted the region's topsoil. In fact, so dry and devoid of moisture had the region become that whenever high winds would blow across the area, the loose and dry sand-like dirt would be picked up and swirled into dense dust storms called "black blizzards." The extended dry period which caused the recurrent dust storms wreaked havoc across the entire region, destroying crops, choking cattle and pasture lands and driving 60% of the population from the area.

The Dust Bowl

The Dust Bowl period illustrates an important point in regard to droughts; the lack of precipitation as the immediate cause of a drought can be intensified by the related activities of man. Actions such as large-scale deforestation, excessive soil erosion, excessive irrigation and over-use of available water sources (such as reservoirs and rivers), and the unintended consequences of infrastructure developments (or changes) by human beings can all exacerbate the effects of a drought beyond what would normally be experienced in their absence. This is especially true when there is no corresponding level of precipitation to replenish existing (or depleted) water levels. In a few extreme cases, the actions of man have been *directly* responsible for regional droughts.

Between 2006 and 2010, the effects of an on-going long-term drought in California were intensified in the Central Valley region of the state by federal policies meant to protect an endangered fish species. As a result of court-backed rulings, the United States Fish & Wildlife Service (USFWS)

> issued what is known as a "biological opinion" imposing water reductions on the San Joaquin Valley and environs to safeguard the federally protected *hypomesus transpacificus*, a.k.a., the delta smelt. As a result, tens of billions of gallons of water from mountains east and north of Sacramento have been channelled [sic] away from farmers and into the ocean, leaving hundreds of thousands of acres of arable land fallow or scorched.[5]

Similarly in 2012-2013, the Maharashtra District in India suffered a drought which severely and adversely affected agricultural production in the region. To make matters worse, the hydrological drought—fueled by less than normal rainfall in the area—was believed to have been made worse by poor irrigation planning, "water management, accompanied by corruption, water-intensive cropping patterns and absence of a long-term view to manage water..."[6]

Unlike a heat wave or a simple "dry spell" (a *limited* period of time without any appreciable rainfall), a drought can potentially cause entire regions almost anywhere in the world to slowly dry out. Taken together, droughts and heat waves are among the top 3 threats to population in the world (along with famine flooding).

A local riverbed in North America, showcasing the effects of a prolonged drought.

---

[5] "California's Man-Made Drought" (2001, September 2) Wall Street Journal, Online edition.

[6] Menon, Meena, (2013 April 3). "Maharashtra Drought Man-Made: Analysis." The Hindu.com

How Do They Form?

Like many other examples of extreme weather, heat waves require a particular set of atmospheric conditions as well as specific weather "ingredients" in order to form. Droughts on the other hand tend to be predicated on a set of meteorological as well as environmental variables, usually initiated by the absence of normal amounts of precipitation.

Heat waves over the U.S. tend to form when air masses form over regions that provide abundant sources of humidity, such as over the Gulf of Mexico or the Caribbean Sea. Carried by the jet streams high in the atmosphere, these hot air masses begin to form high-pressure systems over different regions of the country, particularly in areas east of the Rocky Mountains. Since weather patterns in the warmer weather months are not as susceptible to rapid changes as those in the cooler months, mid-level high pressure tends to move more slowly.   Under high pressure, the air is forced toward the surface, forming an atmospheric "dome" which helps to trap summertime heat instead of allowing it to dissipate. Over time, the trapped air strengthens and stagnates over a region for several days or longer. Under these conditions, both cloud formation and rain becomes extremely difficult to form. The end result is a continual build-up of heat at the surface that we experience as a heat wave.

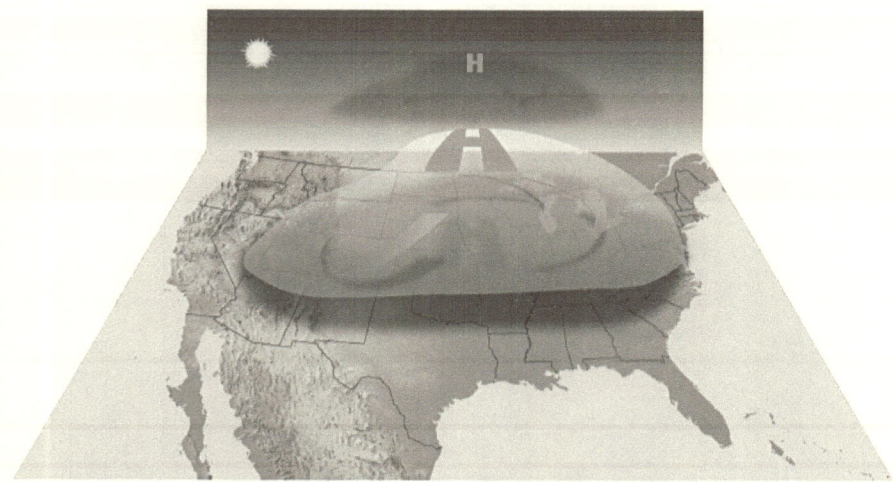

High pressure in the middle layers of the atmosphere acts as a dome or cap allowing heat to build up at the earth's surface.

Heat waves and droughts have both similar and different characteristics due to the fact that they are often associated with one another. At times they may occur simultaneously, one caused or sustained by the other. But it's not uncommon for one to be present independently of the other, based on separate meteorological triggers. However, whereas heat waves tend to be relatively short-term occurrences, droughts tend to be lengthy events with a greater environmental impact. Additionally, droughts are usually the result of extended weather patterns, rather than the passing changes in weather that spawn heat waves.

Although somewhat difficult to both predict and understand, droughts are usually associated with "large-scale upper-air waves, the jet stream flow patterns, and subtropical high-pressure systems,"[7]

Polar Jet
Subtropical Jet

Jet streams carry weather systems and affect the earth's weather patterns. Note how warmer weather tends to be confined below particular jet stream patterns.

Insomuch as North American droughts are concerned, the particular jet stream that affects the weather patterns over the entire continent tend to be typically located *above* the area prolonged dryness. Existing high-pressure systems in the North Atlantic and Pacific oceans will often converge with existing highs over the adjacent continental landmass to form a dry stagnant pattern around the region that the drought will develop. This convergence of weather systems will result in a number of things. First, any moisture from above or below the system will be directed around the system itself, keeping the region dry. Second, resulting clear skies sustained by the now stationary high pressure system will keep the region warm.

The uninterrupted warm and dry weather will then result in a dry and warm ground. Heat emitted from the warm ground will, in turn, prolong these weather conditions prevents by retarding the evaporation process. This allows the ground to absorb more of the energy from the sun, sending more heat into the atmosphere, creating a cycle of chronically dry conditions.

The presence of drought-relevant meteorological elements—high-pressure weather systems, the location of the jet-streams, and the behavior of contributing air waves—are part of the natural flow of ever-shifting weather changes that take place every day throughout every year. To this effect, impending and/or occurring droughts are simply a matter of the chance convergence of necessary weather patterns. But the chance blending of the relevant weather patterns that give rise to droughts are also linked to a set of semi-cyclical meteorological phenomena related to ocean temperatures. The alternating warming and cooling patterns of the oceans—as they relate to their effect on global weather patterns, including droughts—are known as *El Nino* (el neen-yoh) and *La Nina* (Neen-yuh) respectively.

El Nino

The ocean-based meteorological phenomenon dubbed "El Nino"[8] by *climatologists* (scientists who specialize in studying the earth's climate and its environmental impact) is the warming of the surface water temperatures in area of the eastern and central Pacific Ocean (near the earth's equator). When an El Nino ocean-weather pattern develops, the resulting warmer waters of the Pacific will pump more

---

[7] Bob Rauber, John Walsh, Donna Charlevoix. Severe and Hazardous Weather: An Introduction to High Impact Meteorology (2012).

[8] El Nino - Spanish for "The Boy," is an allusion to the December-celebrated Christian Christ-child birth. It is also a reference to the timing of this phenomenon, as it usually takes place in intervals between every 3-7 tears around the period leading up to the Christmas holiday.

moisture into the air. This causes a greater number of intense rain storms—showers, thunderstorms and tropical storms—over a much larger area than in periods where ocean waters remain in at average temperatures. This increases the occurrence of inclimate weather over areas, creating weather systems that affect areas in the middle latitudes across North America. This setup causes moisture-bearing storms to be shifted away from these areas. This is due to the dramatic weakening of the trade winds that cause a shifting in the major wind currents, including the jet streams. These altered wind currents, which normally steers normal weather patterns across the Pacific, results in short-and intermediate-term climate changes that have—in the past—have been observed bringing drought conditions to places such as Australia, Africa, India, and in the central and Eastern U.S. In addition, El Nino events can also be the cause for heat waves in these potentially affected regions, as precipitation levels tend to be reduced.

La Nina

La Nina is the ocean-based meteorological opposite of El Nino. Whereas El Nino is a warming of large surface areas of the central Pacific Ocean, La Nina[9] is a cooling of the ocean surface that tends to result in cooler-than-normal temperatures. During La Nina events, the drought potential in the U.S. tends to shift toward parts of the West, the Southwest, and Southeastern regions of the country. Similar shifts in drier weather can also affect regions in and around equatorial East Africa, and coastal regions of Peru and Chile. It has been thought that most of the major droughts of the 20th century—the Dust Bowl of the 1930s, the harsh dry spells in the Southwest of the 1950s, and the intense drought of 1998-2002— have corresponded to La Nina events.

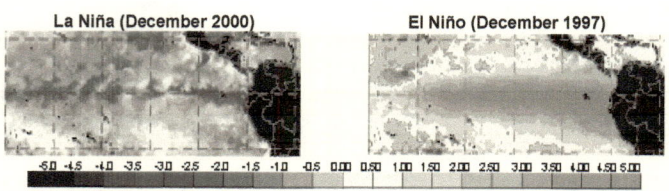

Sea surface temperature of relevant Pacific Ocean waters comparing La Nina to El Nino (in Celsius).

Depending on where one resides and their respective durations, heat waves and droughts can be a temporary disruption of comfort, a short-term emergency situation, or an extended threat to health and/or even life. However, every summer season in a given region is not guaranteed to have a heat wave, just as every year will not yield a drought. But, just as with any extreme weather event, an occurrence of either of these particular extremes is always a possibility. This is especially true in the case of El Nino- and La Nina-event years. For this reason, it is important for individuals to keep abreast of long-term weather forecasts—especially for those whose economic livelihoods depend on the weather, such as farmers and those who routinely work outdoors (see the next section).

---

[9] The name La Nina is derived from the Spanish, which translates into "the girl"—the opposite of El Nino meaning "the boy."

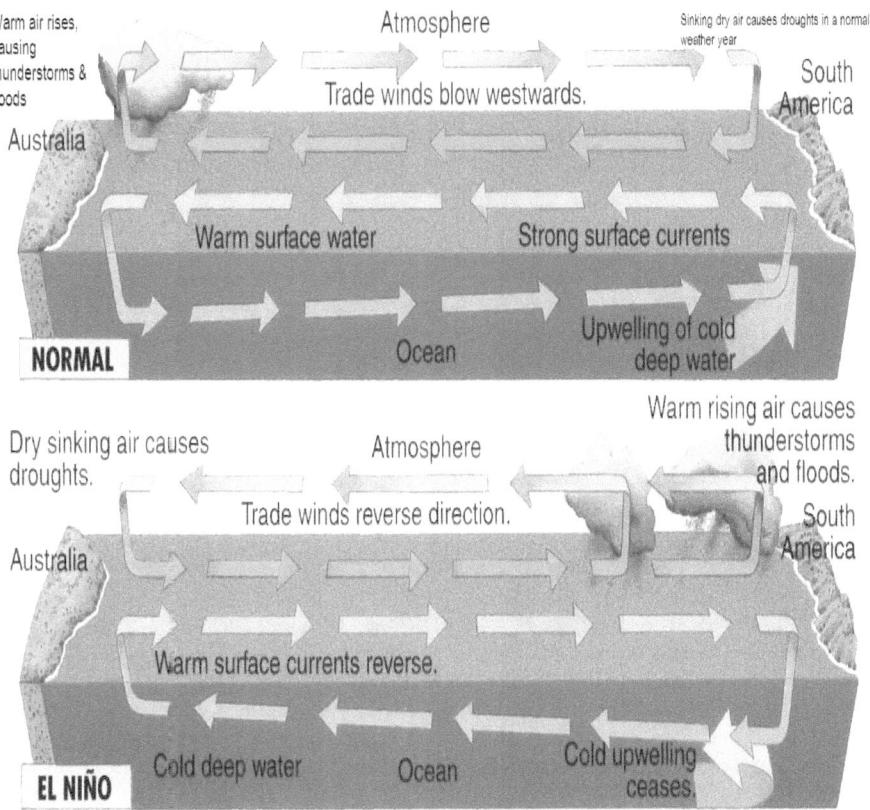

An illustrated comparison of relevant wind and ocean temperature patterns in a normal weather year versus a year where an El Nino-event is present. In the above graphic, the ocean-weather patterns would affect drought potential on the Australian and South American continents.

What Makes Heat Waves Dangerous?

In regions of the world where the transitions of seasons occur, summer temperatures can variate between normal and exceptionally hot. These regions include the United Kingdom, parts of Central Europe, Australia, and the northern two-thirds of the North American continent. In all likelihood, some areas within these regions will see at least several successive days a year when the temperatures will exceed the yearly average and create dangerous heat-related health concerns. Similarly in the U.S., most (but not all) summers will see heat waves in one or more parts of the country. And in areas east of the Rocky Mountains, heat waves tend to combine both high temperature and high humidity although some of the worst heat waves have been catastrophically dry). What's more, when temperatures soar for extended periods of time, they can affect aspects of a populated region's infrastructure. They can also create related economic losses when a region's infrastructure—as well as private property of individuals—is affected.

In the U.S., excessive heat-related injuries and illnesses are the single greatest weather-related causes of death, resulting in hundreds of fatalities each year. In fact, on average, excessive heat claims more lives each year than floods, tornadoes and hurricanes combined. During the historic 1980 heat wave that affected the central and eastern U.S., an estimated 1,000 – 1,300 people died as many states experienced weeks of temperatures in the triple-digits (100°+Fahrenheit). Making the heat wave of 1980 worse was for the fact that it occurred in the midst of a record-setting drought during the same period. In another equally-historic heat-related event, a heat wave that affected the U.S.'s Midwestern region in 1995 resulted in more than 700 deaths. Most of these deaths were among poor and elderly residents living in the city of Chicago forced to endure temperatures in excess of 100 degrees—without the relief of air-conditioning—for nearly a week.[10]

On a few rare occasions, heat waves may set exceptional records in both intensity and casualty rates. From late October of 1923 to early April of the following year, the town of Marble Bar, located in Western Australia set the modern record for the longest number of consecutive days above 100°F (38 °C). The Marble Bar heat wave of 1923-24 lasted a total of an astounding 160 days, setting a benchmark for extreme heat waves. Another, more contemporary example of an extreme heat wave took place across the European continent in 2003. For several weeks between July and August, relentlessly hot temperatures soared in several countries, including the United Kingdom, Belgium, Germany, and the Netherlands. Estimates range from 30,000 – more than 50,000 casualties, with an estimated 14,000 occurring in France alone. Just as in the 1996 Chicago Heat Wave, most of those who perished in France were elderly and those already suffering from ill-health.

So why do so many people die from exposure to extreme heat? What makes hot weather—and in particular heat waves—the leading cause of weather -related deaths annually? For starters, most of the dangers inherent in hot weather stem from the effects of our uninterrupted exposure to high

---

[10] Contributing to the particularly death-toll in the Chicago Heat Wave of 1995 was the phenomenon known as the "urban-island heat-effect," discussed in greater depth on page 39.

temperatures. During extremely hot and humid weather, the body's ability to cool itself can be easily compromised. Under these conditions, when the body fails to cool itself properly, when it heats up too rapidly to cool itself, or when too much of our bodily fluids (i.e., water) or salt is lost through dehydration or sweating , body temperature rises and heat-related illnesses may develop. Since humidity is a key player in most weather, the high relative humidity that often accompanies hot weather and heat waves plays an important part in heat-related illnesses.

Health Concerns

Humidity

The presence of high relative humidity during hot weather/heat waves has the effect of raising the overall discomfort level in human beings (and animals) higher than what would normally be experienced on days with lower humidity levels. This is because the higher the level of humidity, the higher the air temperature actually feels to the human body. The combination of how both heat and humidity feels to our bodies has been studied and quantified by weather experts. In fact, the estimated comfort/discomfort level expected during extremely hot weather has been added to most daily forecasts in the form of the "heat index," a quantified measurement of this potentially deadly combination used by the United States' National Weather Service (NWS).

The *heat index* is an index (i.e., "guide") that combines air temperature and relative humidity in an attempt to determine the apparent effect of high temperatures on our bodies—how hot it feels (Canadian meteorologists utilize a similar index known as the *humidex*, a blend of the two words "humidity" and "index"). To illustrate the index's application, when the humidity level is high, and the outdoor temperature is 90°F (32 °C), the heat index calculates that the apparent temperature (feels) to be about 106 °F (41 °C). However, this calculation of the heat index presumes how it feels under such condition in shady conditions; exposure to full sunshine can increase heat index values by up to 15°F.

National Weather Service
Heat Index
Temperature (°F)

Relative Humidity (%)	80	82	84	86	88	90	92	94	96	98	100	102	104	106	108	110
40	80	81	83	85	88	91	94	97	101	105	109	114	119	124	130	136
45	80	82	84	87	89	93	96	100	104	109	114	119	124	130	137	
50	81	83	85	88	91	95	99	103	108	113	118	124	131	137		
55	81	84	86	89	93	97	101	106	112	117	124	130	137			
60	82	84	88	91	95	100	105	110	116	123	129	137				
65	82	85	89	93	98	103	108	114	121	128	136					
70	83	86	90	95	100	105	112	119	126	134						
75	84	88	92	97	103	109	116	124	132							
80	84	89	94	100	106	113	121	129								
85	85	90	96	102	110	117	126	135								
90	86	91	98	105	113	122	131									
95	86	93	100	108	117	127										
100	87	95	103	112	121	132										

Likelihood of Heat Disorders with Prolonged Exposure or Strenuous Activity

☐ Caution   ☐ Extreme Caution   ■ Danger   ■ Extreme Danger

The Heat Index Chart shaded zone above 105°F (darker shades) shows a level that may cause increasingly severe heat disorders with continued exposure or physical activity.

What's more, winds carrying hot dry air can add heat to the body.

Taking the application of the heat index into consideration, when the outdoor temperatures reach the same level of normal temperature of the human body (approximately 98°F, 36°C), our bodies automatically react in an effort to keep us feeling cool. Our skin begins to excrete sweat, the rate and depth of our blood circulation begins to change, and our respiration increases—all in an effort to cool our body down. However, sweating can only successfully cool the body down if the water—a major component of sweat—is able to evaporate through the skin. But the presence of high relative humidity along with high temperatures often affects the rate at which the water can evaporate from the skin. When the air contains a high rate of moisture (which one finds on days in which the humidity levels are high), it becomes harder for the air to absorb any more moisture, including the moisture from the sweat of our skin. When this happens, the process of sweating can no longer effectively cool our bodies down; our bodies continue to heat up. Overheating becomes a real probability under such circumstances. When our bodies overheat, we lose water and chemicals that the body needs, leading to dehydration and chemical imbalances within the body. The result is that our bodies not only feel hotter (as reflected in the heat index), but actually become hotter as they forced to do other things to cool us down.

Dehydration depletes the body of water needed for sweating. It also causes the blood to thicken, requiring more pressure to pump it through the body. This increased effort to cope with the high temperatures and humidity combination places a strain on the heart and blood vessels. As blood goes to the external surface of the body, less goes to the muscles, the brain, and other organs. When our bodies become so affected by hot weather, any level of heat-related illnesses can result.[11] Heat-related illnesses can range from heat rash to the more serious heat stroke.

Heat Rash

Heat rash is the most common problem in hot environments. Also known as "prickly heat" and *miliaria*, heat rash is a common enough heat-related affliction among infants. However, heat rash can

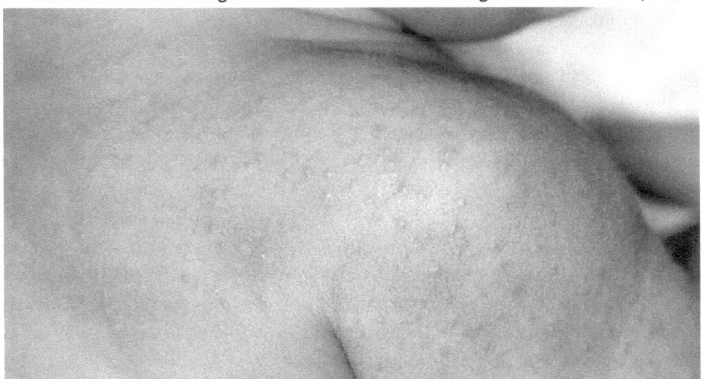

also affect adults, particularly during hot, humid weather. Heat rash develops when the body's sweat ducts — commonly referred to as "pores" — become blocked with excess sweat. This sweat (or "perspiration") then becomes trapped in the skin. When this happens, the skin above the area where the perspiration is unable escape becomes irritated beneath the skin. This irritation can cause the skin to become inflamed and form patches of blisters that can appear as red-colored lumps, or as a cluster of pimples clusters. Heat rash usually appears on the neck, upper chest, in the groin, under the breasts and in elbow creases. It also appears often on the shoulder area. What's more, some forms of heat rash can be intensely itchy or cause a prickly feeling.

Although heat rash usually goes away on its own, severe forms of heat rash may need medical care. But the best way to relieve symptoms is to cool the affected area(s) of the skin and prevent sweating. Treatment of possible heat rash:

• Those affected by a suspected case of heat rash should relocate to a cooler, less humid work environment.
• The rash area should be kept dry. A fan may be used to dry the skin off faster and to reduce sweating.
• Reduce friction to the affected area. Loose clothing should be worn to prevent irritation caused by clothing that rubs against the skin.
• Powder may be applied to increase comfort.
• Ointments and creams should not be used on a heat rash. Anything that makes the skin warm or moist may make the rash worse.
• Treat fever. On a few rare occasions, heat rash may be accompanied by a fever. Any fever should be

---

[11] Such effects are more pronounced, and more dangerous, depending on age and overall physical condition (including the presences of any preexisting health issues). Even individuals who are relatively healthy, but unaware of the effects of increased physical exertion in dangerously hot and conditions, are also at risk.

treated with an over-the-counter drug, like acetaminophen or ibuprofen.

Fortunately, it is not difficult to prevent cases of heat rash during hot and humid weather. The best way is to avoid situations that can lead to excessive sweating. If possible, individuals should remain in a cool setting indoors, particularly on hot humid days and/or during heat waves. Drinking plenty of cold fluids on hot days helps keep the body hydrated. Strenuous physical activity and/or exercise should be avoided during these conditions, as they will likely result in excessive sweating. In hot weather, the use air conditioning, fans, and cool showers is highly advised to help cool the body. In the cases of cold showers and baths, the skin should be dried thoroughly. Finally, wearing lightweight and loose-fitting clothing helps keep limit the probability of sweating.

Sunburn

Sunburn is the direct result of the skin's overexposure to *ultraviolet radiation* (UV)[12] emitted from the sun. In essence, it is a slow burning of the outermost layer of skin that is exposed to more of the sun's UV rays than it can handle. Sunburn can vary from mild to severe. The extent depends on skin type of the person being exposed, and amount of exposure to the sun. The body natural defense against excessive sunlight, *melanin[13]* (the pigment which gives color to our skin, hair, and parts of our eyes) gets overwhelmed, as it becomes incapable of producing enough of the pigment to prevent UV rays from damaging blood vessels close to the skin's surface. Continual sunburn is also a serious risk factor for skin cancer, as severe sun burns tend to cause irreparable damage resulting from accumulations over multiple exposures.

Symptoms of sunburn are well known: the skin becomes red, painful, and abnormally warm after lengthy sun exposure. In many cases, the surface of the burned area of exposed skin feels warm to the touch (compared to the unexposed skin). This feeling of increased warmth generally stems from the increase in blood flow to the exposed areas of skin. And the discomfort associated with sunburn is usually minor, with healing occurring in about a week. But several days before the skin fully heals, the exposed areas may start to heal itself by the spontaneously "peeling" the top layer of damaged skin. After peeling, the skin may temporarily have an irregular discolored appearance. And as in the case of heat rash, more severe sunburn may require medical attention. [14]

---

[12] Although UV rays make up only a very small portion of the otherwise broad radiation spectrum of energy released by the sun, they are the primary cause of sunburn's damaging effects on the skin. Two types of ultraviolet radiation, "UV-A" (long-wave rays) and "UV-B" (short-wave rays), damage the skin, ages it prematurely, and increases risk of skin cancer in those experiencing repeated and/or long-term exposure. See: Appendix A for a more in-depth explanation of ultraviolet radiation.

[13] Melanin is produced by Melanocytes, which are specialized skin cells located in the lower part of the outermost layer of skin.

[14] See: Appendix B for supplemental information on sunburn, including degrees and/or types of burns.

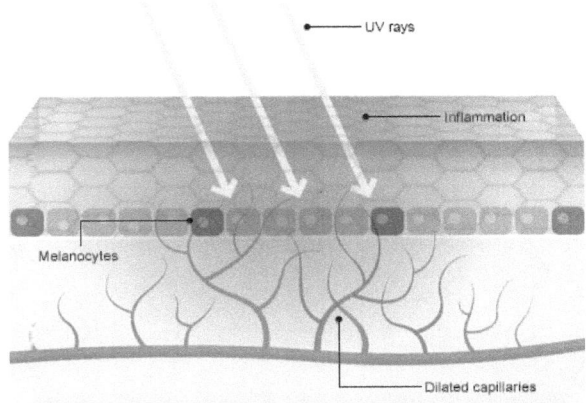

In order to help judge the length of time by which an individual can safely remain outdoors—in full sunlight—given the estimated potency of the sun's rays on a given day, scientists developed the UV Index. This index, which was adopted officially the NWS and the Environmental Protection Agency (EPA), provides a daily projection of the expected risk of overexposure to the sun. The Index calculates the risk of overexposure to the sun's rays by taking into account factors such as cloud coverage and other local conditions that affects the amount of UV radiation reaching the ground in a given part of the country (or the world). The Index predicts UV intensity levels on a scale of 1 to 11+, where 1 indicates a low risk of overexposure and 11+ signifies an extreme risk.

UV Index	Description	Recommended Protection	Sun Burn Time
0-2	No danger to the average person	Wearing a Hat and/or Sunglasses is Sufficient	1 Hour+
3-5	Little risk of harm from unprotected sun exposure	Wear a Hat and Sunglasses. Use SPF 15+ Sunscreen	40 Minutes
6-7	High risk of harm from unprotected sun exposure	Wear a Hat and Sunglasses. Use SPF 30+ Sunscreen. Cover the Body With Clothing. Avoid the Sun if Possible.	30 Minutes
8-10	Very high risk of harm from unprotected sun exposure	Wear a Hat and Sunglasses. Use SPF 30+ Sunscreen. Cover the Body With Clothing. Avoid the Sun if Possible.	20 Minutes
11+	Extreme risk of harm from unprotected sun exposure	Take All Precautions Possible. It is Advised to Stay Indoors.	Less Than 15 Minutes

The amount of UV exposure a person gets depends on the strength of the rays, the length of time the skin is exposed, and whether the skin is protected with clothing. Several other factors may affect how severe a potential case of sunburn based on the parameters established by the Index. These include:

• Time of day. During the period between 10 am and 3pm, when the sun's rays are most intense (although it is possible to receive enough sun exposure during earlier and later periods to receive sunburn).
• The season. Although it is possible to experience sunburn any time of year—including winter—the summer season is the time of year when most cases are occur.
• Infants, children, and individuals with certain pre-existing health conditions (such as lupus) can be particularly sensitive to the burning effects of the sun.
• Certain medications (such as some antibiotics) can trigger changes in the body, making skin easier to sunburn.
• Location. Regularly warmer regions tend to have higher incidence of sunburn than regions with comparatively milder temperatures. Additionally, the closer to the earth's equator a region is, the higher the incidence of sunburn to exposed skin.
• Terrain/geography. Individuals living in higher elevations can often have an increased risk for sunburn. What's more, the sun's rays are often reflected off surfaces like sand and snow (sand and snow reflect up to 85% of dangerous UV rays, which could actually intensify exposure).

In addition to these factors, there are several other related circumstances one might consider which may increase the likelihood of sunburn. The first is the fact that *any* exposed part of an individual's body— including earlobes, scalp and lips—can experience sunburn. Even areas of the skin that are covered with clothing can burn if, for example, the apparel is made of a loose weave that allows

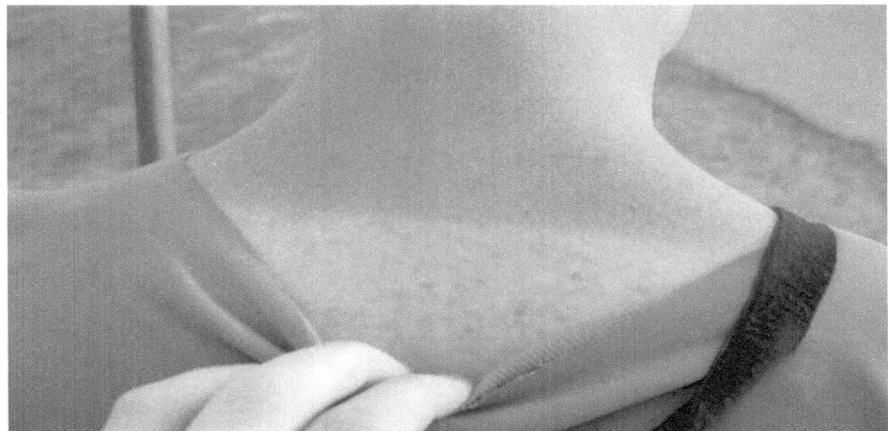

A case of sunburn across the unprotected portion of the neck (photo: courtesy of WYRK.com). Take note of the red discoloration.

ultraviolet (UV) light through. Even unprotected eyes, which are extremely sensitive to the sun's UV light, also can burn (unburned eyes may feel painful or gritty).

Heat Cramps

Heat cramps are painful, brief muscle cramps that tend to occur during exercise or strenuous physical activity in a hot environment, such as those that exist during heat waves, droughts, or similarly hot weather. During heat cramps, muscles in the body may involuntarily jerk or spasm during intense activity...or even a few hours after such activity. And though exertion may also induce cramps in cool weather or in unfit individuals, heat cramps occur in physically fit people who sweat a great deal. These individuals may subsequently drink water to replace fluids lost through the body's sweating process. But bodily salts lost through are not so easily replaced. This loss of the body's salt (and other minerals) can cause, among other conditions, increased cramping in the muscles. And some individuals are more susceptible to this condition than others, including manual laborers (e.g., steel workers, roofers, miners), military trainees, and athletes.

In most cases, the onset of cramping is sudden, usually occurring in muscles of the extremities (arms and legs). Tired muscles—those used for performing the work—are usually the ones most affected by heat cramps. Cramping can begin during or even hours after physical exertion, and may be accompanied by pain and spasms that can be severe enough to incapacitate the hands and feet. What's more, these spasms and any accompanying pain can last for several hours.

Heat Exhaustion

Heat exhaustion is one of the more serious heat-related illnesses, and occurs when the body is no longer able to cool itself off. This is caused primarily by the body's loss of excessive amounts of water and salt contained within sweat. When this happens, the body temperature rises, causing heat-related illness. Heat exhaustion is a condition that results from exposure to high temperatures combined with high humidity, and strenuous physical activity. This condition can also be a precursor of the more serious condition known as *heatstroke* (see next page).

It is important to recognize the symptoms of heat exhaustion in order to properly prevent the condition from worsening. These symptoms include:

- Cool, moist skin that may have a pale appearance (the skin may also be covered with goose bumps as its exposed to heat)
- Heavy sweating
- Dizziness
- Fatigue
- Weak, rapid pulse
- Low blood pressure upon standing
- Muscle cramps
- Slight fever
- Nausea
- Headache
- Feeling weak and/or confused
- Dark-colored urine (an indication of severe dehydration)
- Shallow-rapid breathing
- Fainting linked to high temperatures (also called "heat syncope").

Anyone who physically exerts themselves in very hot weather is potentially at-risk for heat exhaustion. But there are those who possess certain pre-existing health concerns who are at greater risk for the onset of this condition. Those of increased risk include:

- Individuals who do not drink enough water/fluids, particularly in hot weather
- The very young and the very old are especially vulnerable (the elderly and children under 5 years of age)
- Those who suffer from chronic Illnesses or disabilities, especially cardiovascular and respiratory diseases. Those suffering from hypertension/high-blood pressure are also at increased risk (any health condition that causes dehydration makes the body more susceptible to heat sickness).
- Those considered obese (the bodies of overweight people tend to retain more body heat).
- Pregnant women
- Frequently drinkers of alcohol
- Individuals who work physically-demanding jobs such as construction workers, landscapers, athletes, military personnel, etc.00particularly outdoors including in hot weather
- Individuals taking medications that interfere with the body's ability to cool itself, including antipsychotics, some antibiotics, tranquilizers, antihistamines, antidepressants, beta-blockers, and some over-the-counter sleep aids.

<u>Heat Stroke</u>

Without prompt treatment, heat exhaustion can lead to *heatstroke*, a life-threatening condition. In fact, any of the previously listed heat-related ailments can progress to heat stroke if left untreated and exposure to hot and humid conditions continues unchecked. But heat stroke (also known as "sunstroke") can also occur without any of the previous illnesses ever having set in. This condition results from prolonged exposure to high temperatures—usually in combination with high relative humidity and massive loss of fluids through dehydration—that leads to a complete failure of the body's capacity to cool itself off.

During a heat stroke,[15] the body's core temperature rises above the average of 98°F (37°C) to 105°F (40°C) and above; this is to say that the recognized medical threshold for heat stroke is a body temperature of 105° (40°C) degrees or greater. This happens when the body cannot sufficiently dissipate heat, which causes the body's temperature to rise. Dehydration contributes to this sudden rise in body temperatures (which can occur in as little as between 10-15 minutes time) due to the fact that the body of a dehydrated individual may not be able to perspire fast enough to dissipate heat.

Infrastructure Damage

Power Outages

During periods of hot humid weather, the desire for individuals to stay cool becomes a priority; this especially true in cases of prolonged periods of hot days and during heat waves. What's more, the drop in temperatures that normally takes place with the arrival of nighttime cooling is typically absent, due to the physics behind how objects—particularly buildings—retain the heat of the daytime hours. During such periods, the general discomfort level rises, and those affected will usually turn to the use air-conditioners, electric fans and the like in an attempt to stay cool. And as more and more people operate turn to such appliances, more and more electricity is used. Power consumption then spikes. During the peak summertime hours of electrical usage (starting around 3pm in most cases), increased electrical usage places increased power demands on both local and regional power grids, as well as the electrical systems that run them. In some cases, the accumulated demand for electricity by so numerous households and businesses during hot spells can cause power and electrical systems (as well as transmission) lines to overload. These overloads can—and in a few cases, do—result in local or regional power outages ("power blackouts").

Power failures resulting from heat waves are not uncommon, even in highly-developed countries. When these outages occur, the lack of relief from the heat often makes a bad situation worse. In 1988, a two-week heat wave brought temperatures of 120°F (49°C) to the northern, western, and central parts of India. Some 450 deaths resulting from the heat wave were made worse by power outages due to overwhelming demands for electricity. Some of the 700 deaths that occurred during the 1995 Chicago Heat Wave were likewise the direct result of those lacking electrical power when excessive air-conditioner use maxed out the power grid from those seeking to remain cool. During extremely hot, high power usage and [any resulting] power outages are always a possibility. Just as one should prepare

---

[15] Medically speaking, a heat stroke is not an actual stroke in terms of a blood flow blockage within the brain. A "stroke" is the general term used to describe decreased oxygen flow to an area of the brain, as caused by a disruption in oxygen-carrying blood.

before venturing out in the heat, one should prepare for the possibility of a power disruption during such times (see the section, "What to Do in a Heat Wave?" for recommended precautions to take in the event of a power outage).

<u>Material/Physical Damage</u>

In addition to the threatening lives, heat waves can also cause potential damage to an affected area's infrastructure—to roads, railways, bridges, electrical equipment, and so on. This is truer for developed areas more so than for undeveloped areas. In developed countries like the U.S., Canada, and Western European countries, extended periods of hot weather has been observed causing roads to crack and buckle. This happens when pavement begins to expand in the heat. The heated pavement begins to contract during the cooler temperatures of the nighttime hours. Under these conditions, a roadway's surface eventually expands at a joint (i.e., crack), the point where moisture routinely seeps between when it rains. This process weakens the pavement, while the applied heat causes the road to buckle and warp.

Obviously, roads buckling due to high temperatures have immediate dangers to those driving on them. Motorists can not only damage their vehicles, but can potentially be hurt or even killed by extensive road damage caused by heat. In one case, a large sport utility vehicle was sent airborne after hitting a patch of highway that had been damaged in such an instance. Similar heat-related damage can occur on bridges. And repairing such damage can cost governments hundreds of thousands—or even millions—of dollars each year if hot weather lasts an extended period (see the graphic on the following page).

Extreme high temperatures can also cause water lines to burst. Not only are damaged water mains costly for communities to repair, but the decrease in water pressure can be a community safety hazard. The supply of drinking and sanitation water can be disrupted to homes and business. What's more, the lack of water pressure could affect efforts by local fire departments to fight fires should one occur during one of these periods.

Finally, the demand for more and more electricity to power cooling devices during hot weather spells often comes at another cost. Increases in the demand for electrical power to help keep people cool can place a strain on equipment (which has capacity limits). Many power grids and electrical infrastructures, though designed to carry a moderate level of electrical demand, are aged. Because of local budgetary constraints, many electrical supply systems have not been updated, nor have many new ones been built recently in most areas. The result is that increased demands for electrical power—along with increased populations in many urban centers—can place a level of strain on these systems and the transmission lines to the point where both power lines and equipment can be overwhelmed. This can cause system

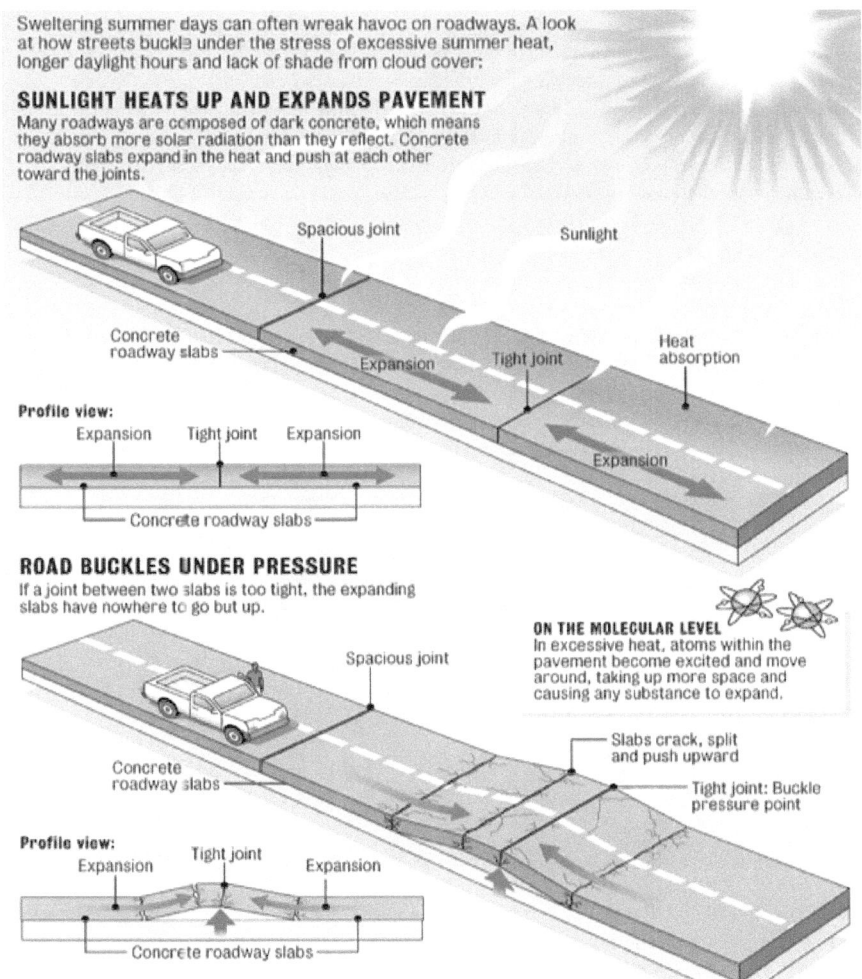

Sweltering summer days can often wreak havoc on roadways. A look at how streets buckle under the stress of excessive summer heat, longer daylight hours and lack of shade from cloud cover:

SUNLIGHT HEATS UP AND EXPANDS PAVEMENT

Many roadways are composed of dark concrete, which means they absorb more solar radiation than they reflect. Concrete roadway slabs expand in the heat and push at each other toward the joints.

Spacious joint

Sunlight

Concrete roadway slabs

Expansion

Tight joint

Heat absorption

Expansion

Profile view:

Expansion   Tight joint   Expansion

Concrete roadway slabs

ROAD BUCKLES UNDER PRESSURE

If a joint between two slabs is too tight, the expanding slabs have nowhere to go but up.

ON THE MOLECULAR LEVEL

In excessive heat, atoms within the pavement become excited and move around, taking up more space and causing any substance to expand.

Spacious joint

Concrete roadway slabs

Slabs crack, split and push upward

Tight joint: Buckle pressure point

Profile view:

Expansion   Tight joint   Expansion

Concrete roadway slabs

A graphic illustrating the mechanics behind how extreme heat can cause damage to roadways failures leading to power outages (i.e., "blackouts"). Power outages can cause major disruptions to daily life—the least of which being the inability to keep cool during heat waves. Blackouts during extreme weather is particularly dangerous for the elderly, as their bodies lack the full capacity to regulate internal temperatures in the same way that younger, more healthy individuals have. A good portion of the more than 700 people who perished during the Chicago Heat Wave of 1995 did so in apartments and homes that lacked air-conditioning, some due to power outages caused by record demands for power during the deadly hot spell.

Environmental Concerns

<u>Wildfires</u>

During heat waves, especially those that occur during droughts (see next section), the increase in temperatures can often combine with the lack of moisture can set the stage for wildfires. This is due to the fact that during long-term periods of uninterrupted high temperatures, land becomes dried out. In these cases, the prevailing dry conditions tend to amplify the probability for fires to start in vulnerable areas. This causes vegetation in the affected areas to become wilted. And dried vegetation becomes

kindling for potential fires that may start from of stray embers (from other fires), a stray lightning bolt occurring in the middle of a field of dried grass, or by the inadvertent actions of human beings (e.g., stray match, a campfire which wasn't extinguished properly, a tossed cigarette, etc.).

Some extreme examples have occurred in recent years in South Australia in January 2009, in Russia in summer 2010, and in Texas and Oklahoma in summer 2011. The record high temperatures in each case, along with the tinder dry conditions, led to extensive wildfires that were extremely costly in terms of lives, structures, human dislocations, and costs.

The No-Nonsense Guide To Heat Wave, Drought, & Hot Weather Safety

What Makes Drought(s) Dangerous?

Generally speaking, droughts stem from a lack of precipitation (i.e., rain) over an extended period of time. This period can be over a series of several weeks, months, several seasons, or even years. Unlike a hot or dry spell, a prolonged lack of rain will cause regions around the world to slowly dry out, and potently affect many more people than a heat wave. This point to one of the two major differences between a heat wave and a drought; droughts tend to be of a longer duration than heat waves, and their impact can be far more extensive. The latter distinction is due to the interplay between the natural event (less precipitation than expected) and the demand people place on water supplies. Furthermore, human activities can exacerbate the impacts of droughts.

Because of their duration and wide-ranging impact, droughts can have significant environmental, agricultural, health, economic and social consequences. These direct effects may vary according to how vulnerable an affected region might be in one aspect of another. This, is turn is based on how developed an affected region is , in addition to how many resources said regions are able to allocate to effectively deal with the related effects of a major drought. For example, developed countries like the U.S., Australia, and others in Europe are better able to mobilize resources to help mitigate the damaging effects on droughts. The more than decade-long drought that occurred in Australia between 1997 and 2009 (also known as the "Millennium Drought") created such a crisis. As a result of that exceptional drought, available water supplies had become so depleted that the country was forced to build a network of desalinization plants to convert ocean salty ocean water into a useful supply for the population. On the other hand, in impoverished countries like those in parts of Asia and Africa, prolonged droughts—in conjunction with the lack of technological and infrastructure development—can have a far more devastating impact. Populations that depend on water availability for farming—and the foods they produce—are far more vulnerable to potential famine caused by drought.

So how and why else are droughts so dangerous? For starters, many of the same heat-related health dangers that can develop during heat waves can also occur during drought, particularly if droughts occur during (or last into) the warmer summer months. As a matter of inevitability, droughts do not always produce heat waves. However, the more prolonged a drought last, the higher the likelihood that both will occur simultaneously at *some* point. But in either case, the dangers and effects involved with droughts can be every bit as long lasting as the event itself.

Health Concerns

Heat-Related Illnesses
Many of the same heat-related illnesses which are a potential hazard during heat waves are also possible during a drought, particularly in the summer months. In fact, heat waves need not be occurring for heat-related injuries to possible; simple hot spells resulting in a particularly hot and humid day can trigger the likelihood for such issues.

Disease
In less-developed areas, the lack of water can impact health in other ways. The lack of water for basic needs such as drinking, public sanitation, and personal hygiene can create a breeding ground for

bacteria that thrive in unsanitary conditions and filth. This can lead to a wide-range of diseases such as cholera, dysentery, and parasitic infections. In areas with fewer resources and weak infrastructures, contracting any number of such diseases can lead to epidemics and can be fatal to large numbers of affected (and infected) individuals.

Thirst/Hunger

Also in underdeveloped regions, the prolonged lack of water can cause widespread thirst, and not just among people. Animals also need water to survive. And without water, animals—a food source for humans—can quickly die off, creating hunger. In searching for adequate supplies of water, animals will often migrate for distances greater than their proximity to human populations, thus adding to the potential for both thirst *and* hunger.

The lack of water in drought conditions also tends to provide too little water to support food crops, especially in areas with limited through irrigation or reserve water supplies. The same problem affects wild-growing grasses and grains used to feed livestock, which free-range animals also graze upon. When drought undermines or destroys food sources, people go hungry. When the drought is severe and continues over a long period, widespread famine may occur. This was the case in the drought that occurred in Northern China between 1959 and 1961, when the world's deadliest famine—trigger by a major drought—caused some estimated 30 million deaths due mostly to starvation.

Environmental Concerns

Wildfires

Just as in the case of a long heat wave, conditions during a drought can—and do—often dry out large swaths of vegetation and plant life. The lack of precipitation that often characterizes droughts can quickly create hazardous conditions in forests and across range lands, setting the stage for wildfires that may cause injuries or deaths as well as extensive damage to property and already shrinking food supplies.

Ecosystem Changes

The potential migration of both human and animals, fueled by the search for both food and water in a drought situation, can have an impact on local ecosystems. Humans and animal species settling in areas where their presence was limited to begin with can alter the feeding and life patterns of prior inhabitants.

Additionally, droughts that last enough to completely dry creek and river beds can cause irrevocable changes to localized ecosystems within affected areas. This is especially true if the affected habitant was the only home to a species of plant and/or animal that is native no other place on the globe. Thus, droughts have the potential to cripple the numbers (or even eradicate the numbers) of an entire species if the effect becomes extensive enough.

Societal Concerns

Unrest

In regions with unstable governments and/or where large portions of said regions have essentially ungoverned land, social conflicts and even war can be triggered by the lack of (or access to) an important resource like water. In such cases, the lack of water and the often corresponding lack of food have been observed contributing to social and even regional tensions among groups and governments competing for limited existing supplies of food and water. Wars that added to mass starvations and thirst have often been the result. Such was scenarios that played out in Ethiopia during the mid 1980s, when almost half a million people perished from famine fueled by both drought and war.

Additionally, mass migrations have also occurred among affected groups of people seeking access to food and water during droughts. When faced with these of drought, many people will flee a drought-stricken area in search of a new home with a better supply of water, enough food, and without the disease and conflict that were present in the place they are leaving.

Where Do Heat Waves/Droughts Occur?

Generally-speaking, both droughts and heat waves can (and do) occur in regions where climates are prone to seasonal patterns. This is to say, these particular weather phenomena tend to occur primarily in and around the planet's *temperate zones*.[16] In geographic al terms, "temperate zones" are those regions in the world that lay both above and below the tropical and the Polar Regions. For the most

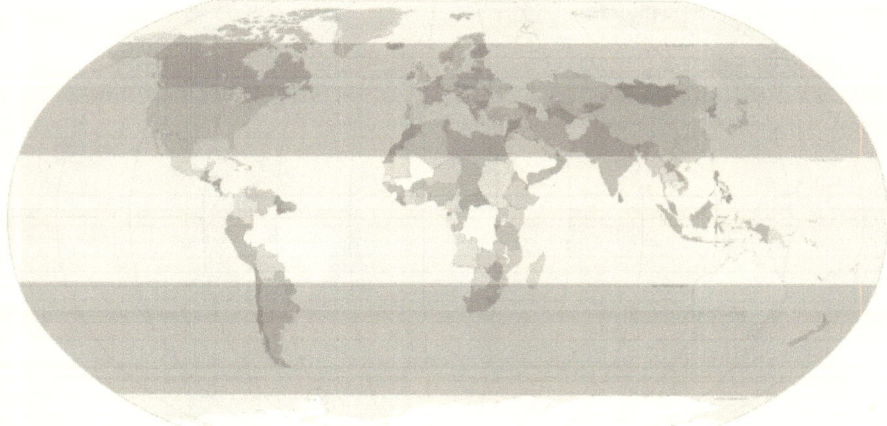

A global map indicating (in the highlighted colors) the earth's northern and southern temperate zone regions, where seasonal weather shifts can occasionally lead to extreme temperature variations (including droughts and heat waves).

part, seasonal changes within temperate zones tend to be moderate rather than extreme. However, on occasion, the variations between summer and winter seasons within these regions can be extreme—depending on weather patterns, and whether or not there is an occurrence of either El Nino or La Nina in (comparatively) nearby ocean waters.

When conditions become favorable for weather extremes, both droughts and heat waves can occur. At times, both can occur simultaneously (and though droughts can produce heat waves, it is rare that heat waves produce droughts—unless it is of such prolonged duration that normal precipitation amounts are adversely affected). And depending on the stubbornness of the particular initiating weather patterns, both heat waves and droughts can last for several weeks; and for months and even multiple seasons in the case of droughts.

---

[16] The fact that droughts tend to occur *primarily* within the temperate zones, this is not meant to imply that they occur *exclusively* within these regions. Many areas in Africa tend to experience droughts, many of which do not fall within either of the temperate zones.

The No-Nonsense Guide To Heat Wave, Drought, & Hot Weather Safety

What to Be On Alert For

Because extremely hot and prolonged weather has its own set of dangers, government agencies charged with monitoring meteorological phenomenon are aware of the importance of keeping the public alert to changes in the weather than could create public hazards. These agencies, particularly those in the U.S. and other developed nations have created a system of hot weather-related advisories—mostly as they relate to heat waves—that alert the public to the probability that high temperatures (and related weather) may adversely affect the public. The NWS and the Meteorological Service of Canada both use a system of hot weather watches and warnings to alert the public in the event of hazardous conditions that may impact health and/or life. These public alerts are as follows:

- Fire Weather Watch[17] – a weather advisory issued to alert local fire and land management agencies (such as a local or regional Resource Department) to the possibility that extremely dry weather conditions conducive to creating a fire hazard are expected in the near future. The watch is issued generally 12 to 48 hours in advance of the expected conditions, but can be issued up to 72 hours in advance depending on the projected accuracy of the general Also, depending on conditions, the watch can be cancelled, allowed to expire, remain in-effect beyond the initial projections of fire hazard conditions, or upgraded to a Red Flag Warning.

- Red Flag Warning - also known as a "Fire Weather Warning," is a forecast warning issued to alert local fire and and management agencies (such as a local or regional Resource Department) that conditions are ideal for the easy ignition of fires, and the ignition and spread of wildfires. A red flag warning is most likely to be issued during drought conditions, when humidity levels are perilously low, the presence of (or significant risk for) lightning, and/or when high or erratic winds are imminent. During red flag warnings, firefighting agencies will alter their staffing and equipment resources dramatically to accommodate the increased forecast risk. To the public at large, a red flag warning means high fire danger with increased probability of a quickly spreading vegetation fire in the area within 24 hours.

- Heat Advisory - is a forecast advisory usually issued within 12 hours of the heat index reaching at least 105°F (40°C), but less than 115°F (46°C) for less than 3 hours per day during a particular period of time. Additionally, a heat advisory is issued when nighttime low temperatures are expected to reach above 80°F (25°C) for 2 consecutive days during the same period.[18] An advisory is issued whenever serious heat-related conditions are anticipated, which can cause significant discomfort or inconvenience and, if caution is not taken, could lead to a threat to life and/or property.

---

[17] In both Fire Weather Watches and Warnings, weather advisories are based on the local vegetation type, topography of the land, and the distance from major water sources the affected fire threat regions are. The calculations also tend to include analyses of daily vegetation moisture content calculations, expected afternoon high temperature, afternoon minimum relative humidity and daytime wind speed. Based on red flag warnings, local law enforcement agencies may initiate bans on outdoor burning (such as campfires and trash burning).

[18] Note: Local weather offices, particularly those where excessive heat is less frequent or in areas with deserts or mountainous terrain, often have their own criteria establishing at what particular point on the heat index a heat advisory may be issued.

- Excessive Heat Watch - is a forecast advisory issued when the heat index is expected to be greater than 105°F (41°C), with nighttime low temperatures will be at least 75°F (24°C) or higher for 2 consecutive days.[19] A Watch is used when the risk of a heat wave has increased, but its occurrence and timing is still uncertain. A Watch provides enough lead time so those who need to prepare can do so, such as cities that have excessive heat event mitigation plans.

- Excessive Heat Warning - is a forecast warning issued within 12 hours of the heat index reaching one of two criteria levels. In most areas, a warning will be issued if there is a heat index of at least 105°F (40°C) for more than 3 hours per day for 2 consecutive days. An excessive heat warning is also issued if the heat index reaches indices greater than 115°F (46°C) for any period of time. High values of the heat index are caused by temperatures being significantly above normal and high humidity, and such high levels can pose a threat to human life through conditions such as heat stroke, heat exhaustion, and other heat-related illnesses. The warning is used for conditions posing a threat to life or property.

Droughts on the other hand, generally do not arrive as suddenly as other natural disasters like hurricanes or tornadoes. The virtual drying up of waterbeds and ground water tends to occur gradually, over a period of time. A drought is said to be underway when an area receives 75% or less of average annual rainfall. Furthermore, drought prediction is somewhat difficult, and can only be done so with a limited range of certainty.

Unlike heat waves or other forms of severe weather, meteorological agencies such as the NWS do not issue urgent weather advisories like *watches* and *warnings* for droughts. Instead, droughts in the U.S are monitored, measured, and quantified by way of the U.S. Drought Monitor. The U.S. Drought Monitor is a weekly[20] analysis of drought conditions for the entire country, the results of which are then mapped out and assigned a severity designation that corresponds to a color-coded map of monitored areas of the U.S. The weekly results of the Drought Monitor are based on measurements of climatic, hydrologic and soil conditions—as well as reported regional impacts and observations from a network of reporting contributors from around the country. Certain agencies of the U.S. government (such as the U.S. Department of Agriculture and the Internal Revenue Service) use the Drought Index to measure, for example, the negative financial impact(s) that ongoing droughts may have on farmers' ability to produce food earmarked for the marketplace. The Index is also used to allocate federal assistance to local municipalities that suffer losses and/or some level of damage from ongoing droughts. Other regions around the world also use a variation of the U.S. Drought Index to likewise monitor and measure the lack of precipitation for their respective regions. The government of Australia, for example issues a monthly drought report by its Drought Watch Service, which is operated by the *National Climate Centre* within its Bureau of Meteorology.

---

[19] The criteria the issuance of an excessive heat watch may vary from region to region. In the Southern U.S. for example, an excessive heath watch is issued only when the heat index is expected to reach at least 110°F (43°C). The same holds true for Canada, where the threshold varies from province to province, and even among different cities—particularly in the province of British Columbia.

[20] U.S. Drought Monitor maps are published every Thursday morning at 8:30 Eastern time, based on data through 7 a.m. the preceding Tuesday. The Monitor is jointly produced by the National Drought Mitigation Center at the University of Nebraska-Lincoln, the United States Department of Agriculture (USDA), and the National Oceanic and Atmospheric Administration (NOAA).

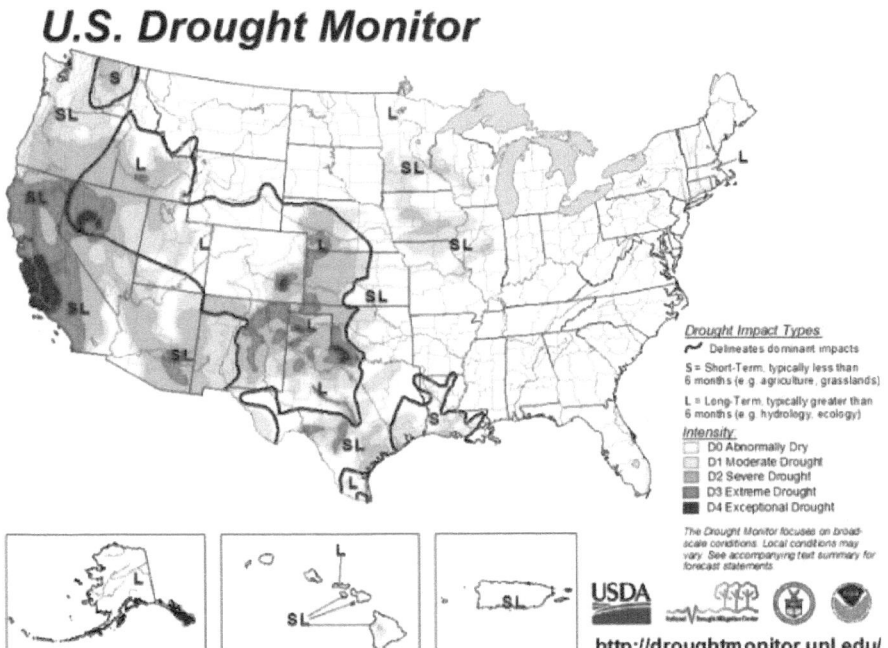

One of the weekly maps published by the U.S. Drought Monitor Index, graphing the effects and severity levels of regional droughts across the continental U.S. Take note of ¯he legend to the right of the map itself that provides an interpretation of drought intensity, represented by color codes (Courtesy: http://droughtmonitor.unl.edu/).

 The lack of precipitation and/or water levels (in ponds, lakes, streams, and rivers) is the primary variable that factors into monitoring drought. Another key measure indicating is the reduction of the moisture content in the soil, which includes ground and well water availability. The general lack of precipitation—that may last for several weeks, months, or entire seasons—tends to have an impact on other aspects of the affected environment. In colder months, a decrease in wintertime precipitation (i.e., snow) and of snowpack on mountain peaks can also contribute to multi-seasonal drought(s). This further contributes to the lack of moisture in the soil indicative of drought conditions, and—whether in warmer or colder months—often gives the ground a dried appearance (see next page for image). And aside from the lack of precipitation, the lack of moisture content in the soil is an indication, particularly to farmers that a drought is underway.

 The lack of either moisture in the soil or appreciable levels of rain will invariably trigger signs of distress in plant life in a drought-affected region. Signs of plant stress include withering or wilting plants (i.e., their leaves), and a lack of growth among the vegetation in an affected region. Another indication among plants that a drought is under-way is a change in their color. Foliage (leaves) will often turn yellow or yellowish-green in color, grass may begin to turn brown, and the leaves of plants will usually die earlier, flowers may fail to bloom, and/or fruit-bearing plants will dispatch their fruits earlier than usual—if at all. This is because the lack of water isn't sufficient enough for the plants to thrive and grow. In many cases, plant roots cannot absorb water normally found in the soil to feed the plants because there is none to be found.

The dried, moisture-deprived appearance of soil during a drought

Animals, particularly those that are a part of farmer livestock, can often suffer from the lack of water and high temperatures often brought on by drought in the same way that human beings can. Cattle and other livestock tend not to feed when temperature—and the general discomfort level—rises to levels of concern. These extreme conditions can also affect the behavior of animals in other ways; cows tend not to give as much milk, while chickens will decrease egg-laying. Cattle may begin bunching together, and exhibiting heavy panting, slobbering, and a general lack of coordination. An increase in animal stress is a warning sign of impending (or occurring) drought.

The No-Nonsense Guide To Heat Wave, Drought, & Hot Weather Safety

What to Do In a Heat Wave and Drought

Heat Waves

Simply put, heat waves can strike any region, any country that experiences warmer-cooler weather seasonal changes. What's more, even areas where cooler climates are the norm can experience abnormally high temperatures that could meteorologically qualify as a heat wave, such as areas of the state of Alaska—an area more regarded for its extreme winters than heat waves. In these regions, many homes do not have air-conditioning, and surviving in the extreme temperatures becomes a challenge for everyone affected.

Heat is the number one weather-related killer in the United States, resulting in hundreds of fatalities each year. On average, excessive heat claims more lives each year than floods, lightning, tornadoes and hurricanes combined. And as with any extreme weather event, preparation is the best form of protection against potential injury...or worse.

Before a Heat Wave/Extreme Heat

Home Preparations

Planning for heat waves and extremely hot weather entails being aware of the potential hazards that can result from such extreme conditions. Hot weather, particularly heat waves are capable of causing heat-related illnesses as well as the loss of electrical power, possible property damage, and general disruptions to daily life.

Homes and other dwellings should be properly prepared for summer heat. A good place to start is to briefly run any air-conditioner (unit) in order to test its operating condition. Also, air-conditioner filters should be changed regularly, while air ducts should undergo a routine cleaning and maintenance check before their use. This is especially true if cooling systems are used on a regular basis (a thorough cleaning or changing of the filters/air ducts every 90 days is a good rule of thumb for cooling systems). Pre-use maintenance of cooling systems can be essential to maximizing the functional efficiency of these units. Blocked air filters and dirty air ducts tend to create a drag on the efficiency of cooling systems, and can impede air flow through a house or dwelling. In rooms with window-mounted air-conditioners, check to see the unit is snug to the window and there are no significant air leaks.

Homes with central air-conditioning should be well sealed to keep cool air from escaping. The condition of the weather-stripping around doors and windows should also be checked. Any air leaks caused by damage to the sealing should be corrected, and damaged dealing should be replaced.

Another way to maximize the use of airflow and to help cool off the interior of homes is to make adjustments to any ceiling fans. During warmer weather, the direction of ceiling fans should be changed to spin in a counter-clockwise direction. This simple adjustment will force airflow downward, producing a chilling-effect in rooms where they operate. Electric (portable) fans can be used to take advantage of air flow during hot weather, but under specific conditions (see the section, "During a Heat Wave/Extreme Heat" for more information on the use of electric fans). To utilize fans to their maximum efficiency, use them in conjunction *with* the air-conditioners.

Windows on the side of dwellings exposed to the sun should be blocked. Pulling down shades, drawing curtains, or shutting any blinds will block sunlight and help keep indoor room temperatures down. However, doing so can also reduce air circulation in homes without air-conditioning. Leaving a gap of space between the shield and the window should help lessen this effect.

An even more effective alternative to blocking sunlight through exposed windows is to install or improvise awnings. Shading windows with the use of awnings can block sunlight without reducing air circulation around windows. Even temporary awnings can be installed using tarps or cardboard. Studies bear this out in that the 'awning effect' can help reduce heat entering a home by as much as 80%.

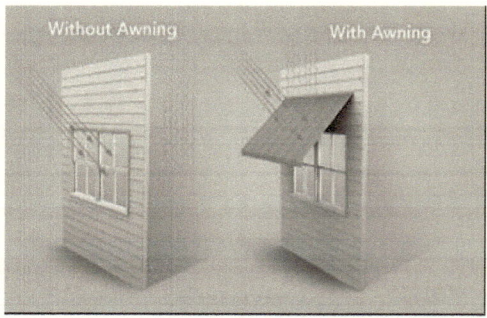

Kitchens are probably the single biggest source of heat inside a home or dwelling, especially during the summer months. This is primarily because the kitchen is where cooking takes place, and majority of appliances used for cooking radiate heat. This heat can travel to other parts of a home, affecting any attempts to keep the interior of a dwelling cool during hot weather. In brief, cooking large meals adds heat to the house. To counter this effect, many foods can be prepared in the early morning or late evening—when the air temperature is cooler. If possible, plan simpler meals during hot weather. But if cooking during hot weather cannot be avoided, using a microwave will help avoid heating up the kitchen.

During hot weather, consuming heavy and/or hot meals actually causes our bodies to become warmer. Meals that require a minimum of cooking, or have some level of pre-preparation involved are the best option to hot heavy meals. Salads and cold fruits like watermelon and cantaloupe are full of water, and will assist in keeping the bodies cool. Sandwiches are also an easy to prepare option, as they can be prepared from cold or room-temperature ingredients.

Emergency Planning

In any extreme weather scenario, keeping abreast of conditions is important. Monitoring local weather forecasts and keeping one's self aware of upcoming temperature changes is perhaps the single best way to do this. Television, radio/weather radio, and internet news sites routinely provide up-to-the-minute updates of weather conditions. Monitoring local forecasts for changes in weather conditions and temperatures are the best barometer by which hot weather contingency plans can be initiated...should the need arise.

The most basic aspect of planning for extreme weather is an honest assessment of what resources are lacking, what's needed, and what resources are available. To illustrate, many homes in under-developed regions, and older homes in developed countries tend not to have air-conditioning. Those who find themselves in such a situation should plan accordingly.

Many large and medium-sized cities in the U.S., Canada, and European countries have contingency plans that include opening "cooling centers" in the event of dangerously hot weather. These centers, designated by local and/or regional governments, are typically places of public accommodation such as schools, public libraries, and shopping centers. The centers generally remain open for as long as the threat of extremely hot weather last. Most major cities in North America and in parts of Europe have established emergency telephone numbers that residents can dial to locate the nearest cooling center.[21] In most cases, these places are usually open to the public during the hottest portion of the day, which makes them a good idea to visit during hot spells...even without their designation as a "cooling center."

Plan to limit the use of electricity during upcoming hot weather periods. Electricity use tends to skyrocket during extremely hot days as people attempt to stay cool. But appliances such as air-conditioners and electric fans—particularly if they are in constant use—tend to use a great deal of electrical energy. And more people using these devices equals more power usage throughout the affected regions. To limit the probability of a region-wide power outage due to massive power usage, plan to turn off and/or unplug any unused appliances or non-vital electrically-powered devices during periods when air-conditioning and other cooling devices are expected to be used. Doing so has the added benefit of keeping utility bills low.

On the subject of heat wave-related power outages, it is best to assume the worst. Consider the possibility that—although a particular household is limiting its power consumption in hot weather—other homes and business may be exceeding recommended power usage. Such a scenario means that a power outage during peak usage hours, typically the hottest part of the day, is a very real likelihood. Anticipating and planning for such an occurrence may make the difference between remaining relatively safe during an extreme weather event, and experiencing a life-threatening heat-related illness. Purchasing or creating a custom hot-weather emergency kit may lessen the chance that a bad situation might be made worse by failing to anticipate needs in an emergency.

Among the essential supplies a hot weather emergency kit should contain are:

Foodstuffs:

- In the majority of cases, trying to estimate how long a power outage might last is simply impossible, as each outage has its own particular set of exact causes, different extents of damage, and locations of the particular malfunction that lead to the outage. Also in most cases, particularly in outages that last for an extended period, refrigerated food can spoil. In anticipation of a long period (of time)without electrical service, a 1-2 day supply of non-perishable, no refrigeration-required food should be packed away somewhere inside or near the

[21] In many parts of Canada and in many U.S. cities, the telephone number to locate cooling centers is 311, while in some areas, the number is 211. Learn the established emergency telephone number for your particular area in the event of a heat emergency.

35

home or dwelling itself in the event of loss of power. Additionally, the foods selected for storage should be of the type that are tightly sealed, requires very little or no preparation (i.e., cooking) and little or need for water. Ideally, food products with similarly close expiration dates should be purchased and stored together, so as to make replacing them at the same time easier if they expire before use.

If storage space availability is limited, consider purchasing military-style Meals Ready to Eat (MRE) packet from surplus or camping stores. MREs are small packets of food rations that require just a little water or maybe some heat to prepare. For foods that don't require cooking, keep track of their individual expiration dates.

- Canned meats such as tuna and beef (jerky) have extended storage lives, so such items should be a main staple of any stored food (unless there are vegetarians present, in which case canned vegetables should be included).
- High energy food sources such as protein, energy, and/or granola bars are idea for storage. They require less space than canned foods, even those that don't require preparation.
- Bottled water. Stored in sealed plastic bottles, bottle water keeps amazingly well for extended periods. The U.S. Food and Drug Administration (FDA) estimates that most bottled water has a potentially indefinite shelf life, so replacing drinking water to should not be a major concern. Ideally, one gallon of water per person, per day should be stored for emergencies. However, Nursing and/or pregnant women, children, and individuals with pre-existing medical conditions might need more water.
- Canned juices, milk, and/or soup (milk and soup can be purchased in powered form, and as such tend to have long shelf lives. Extra water should be considered if powdered foods are going to be used).
- Crackers, cookies, and other ready-to-eat snack foods add variety as well as supplement the food supply.

Supplies/Communication:

- A battery-powered or rechargeable flashlight, penlight, or long-period glow sticks.
- A cell phone, computer tablet, of other device with internet-access capabilities. This may be necessary in order to keep abreast of important news or emergency updates issued by public officials.
- An empty ice chest/container (styrofoam will suffice, but a more solidly-constructed container, such as one composed of solid plastics is better).
- A battery-powered radio for keeping updated on vital information or instructions. A better alternative might be to consider purchasing one of the types of portable radios that rely on neither batteries nor electricity. These units are powered by cranking a handle, which charges a miniature generator inside the unit enough to power it *without* batteries or electricity for a limited amount of time.
- A non-electric/hand-powered can-opener (if not a function of a multi-purpose tool).
- A pack of batteries, preferably an assorted pack containing multiple sizes for battery-powered instruments (e.g., radio).

- Plastic utensils, paper plates, and/or Tupperware or plastic containers (with lids) for serving food.
- Sanitation supplies, including anti-bacterial soap and/or hand sanitizer.
- A first-aid kit. First-aid kits of varying degrees of items can be purchased at mostly any "big box" store, or can be created from scratch based on anticipated needs. At the very least, an effective first-aid kit should contain bandages (the plastic adhesive, rolled cloth, and/or the "liquid" varieties), roller cloth bandages, sterile gauze pads, towelette wipes, medical tape, a liquid antiseptic (e.g., alcohol and/or peroxide), anti-bacterial soap, smelling salts, petroleum jelly, latex gloves, tweezers, scissors, a thermometer, and aspirin or some other pain-reliever.
- Sunscreen, with an effective SPF level (at least 15) in the event that outdoor activities.
- A small, portable electric generator, in the event that electrical power is lost for an extended period of time.

Along with preparing supplies, a common closet or place of storage within the home should be a designated and understood to be a place to access emergency supplies in case of need. In the event of a power loss, common knowledge of this closet's location will make it easier to locate and secure supplies if needed.

During a Heat Wave/Extreme Heat

Indoors

Fortunately over the past several decades of our understanding of meteorology, weather forecasters have become very proficient at determining the arrival of extremely hot weather. As such, it can be vitally important that those who live in regions where extremely hot weather is a reality to be aware of changing temperatures and conditions.

The best way to keep informed about impending hot temperatures is by way of a weather radio. These special radios are designed to broadcast up-to-the-minute weather information from government weather forecast centers. This information may contain short- and long-term weather forecasts, weather alerts, and temperature projections for a given broadcast area. In many cases, these radios can provide early warning of extreme weather changes.

In lieu of a weather radio, traditional broadcast radios can provide nearly as much up-to-the-minute information on changing weather conditions—albeit with less frequency. What's more, many radio stations broadcast internet-based live streams that can be accessed on computers, smart phones, and computer tablets with internet access. And television-based news programs have always—and continue—to incorporate weather updates into their broadcasts.

Unnecessary ventures outside should be avoided. Remaining indoors during the hottest portion of the day is the best way to stay cool...and prevent heat-related illnesses due to extended exposure to heat and humidity. The coolest place in most buildings is the lowest floor; in buildings that have them, basements and/or be ow-ground rooms are the coolest locations. This is because hot air typically rises and cooler air is heavier. This natural flow of air is why attics and upper floors of most homes tend to be hotter than their lower floors and any underground sections.

If possible, use air-conditioning to stay cool while indoors. But as such appliances require a high degree of electrical power to operate them; it's a good idea to turn off all nonessential and unused appliances and electrically-operated conveniences such as lights, computers, televisions, and other such equipment. This also helps to keep overall indoor temperatures somewhat cooler. In addition, doing so also helps to reduce electric power usage, and decreases the likelihood of power outages.

Electric fans can be a limited source of cooling indoors during hot weather periods. Circulating air can cool the body by increasing the evaporation rate of any perspiration. Electric fans can help move the air around indoors, particularly at night when cooler air is pulled inward from outside (provided the fan sets in a window). However, electric fans have limits. A fan will not prevent heat-related illnesses when the temperatures exceed about 90°F (32°C). During the heat of the day, a cool shower is a much more effective way to cool off when temperatures exceed 90 degrees.

If a home is not equipped with air-conditioning, those in need of a cooler place to take shelter should consider relocation to a more comfortable environment. The next best option is to consider spending the warmest part of the day in public buildings such as libraries, schools, movie theaters, shopping malls and other community facilities. In extreme heat emergencies, many local governments will open these places as temporary "cooling centers" in order to help reduce the chance of heat illnesses.

While indoors, simple activities such as eating and drinking can actually raise the body's temperature. Specifically, eating large meals—especially those that are protein-rich—can increase the body's metabolic rate, and therefore raise the body's temperature. These types of meals should be avoided in favor of light and more-balanced meals during hot weather. Alcoholic beverages and caffeine-based drinks should also be avoided as well, as both of these substances can cause frequent urination—and promote dehydration.

On this note, drinking adequate levels of water, fruit juices, or sports drinks becomes all the more important for hydration. In fact, it may become necessary to consume more water than usual when it becomes uncomfortably hot. Also, heavy sweating increases the need to replace vital bodily minerals (such as salts). The best way to accomplish this is to eating small amounts along with food water (or a specially-formulated electrolyte replacement drinks) **before** thirst sets in order to prevent hydration.[22]

Outdoors

Potential threats due to extreme heat can vary, depending on when and where these conditions exist. For instance, though dangers such as heat-related illnesses are just as much if a threat in rural and undeveloped areas as they are elsewhere, such dangers are amplified when location and other factors come into play. Consequently, people living in urban areas may be at greater risk from the effects of prolonged heat spells than those living in rural areas. This may be due in part to factors such as the quality of air found over heavily-populated urban areas (compared to the lack of stagnant air over rural areas). Also, asphalt- and concrete-covered ground stores heat longer, and only gradually releases heat at night. This can produce higher nighttime temperatures from what's known as the "*urban heat island effect.*"

---

[22] Persons who (1) have epilepsy, heart, kidney or liver disease, (2) are on fluid restrictive diets or (3) have a problem with fluid retention should consult a physician before increasing their consumption of fluids.

The No-Nonsense Guide To Heat Wave, Drought, & Hot Weather Safety

As day-time temperatures heat up the hardened surfaces of large cities, this heat-effect phenomenon causes heat to radiate (i.e., reflected) from these surfaces. The result is an increase in the average temperature in cities of up to 10-15 degrees compared to rural and less-developed surrounding areas. What's more, these higher temperatures tend to linger after dark. Therefore, those residing in higher-threat urban areas need to be particularly cognizant of heat-related dangers—especially if going outside cannot be avoided.

Ideally, any activities that might normally take place outdoors should be postponed until a cooler (i.e., later) time of the day. However, if going outside is not an option during hot weather, precautions should be taken. The first is to wear the appropriate level of dress for the conditions. The overall point is to dress enough to cover any exposed areas of the body, while ensuring the body stays relatively cool. Those who need to be outdoors should cover as much as the skin as possible to avoid sunburn. Loose-fitting, lightweight clothing made up of natural materials are best. Avoid wearing materials such as polyesters and flannels, as these fabrics tend to retain sweat. Light-colored clothing should be worn as opposed to dark-colored materials (dark colors tend to absorb head, while lighter colors reflect both heat and light). Protecting the head is also important if outdoors. A wide-brimmed sun hat not only covers the head, but provides a measure of shade around the head area. A moderate-level SPF sunscreen—applied generously—should also be worn along with protective clothing (see below).

Strenuous physical activity (such as exercise or work) should be curtailed, particularly during the hottest portions of the day. However, for individuals who *must* work in such extreme temperatures, the dangers inherent in over-exertion cannot be overstated. For this reason, those who must engage in demanding activity should pace themselves while working. This means taking frequent breaks that include consistently rehydrating themselves with water or other recommended drinks. To ensure personal safety, those who have to work outdoors should do so with a partner. A good practice while engaging in physical activity is to breathe through the nose instead of the mouth. This helps to avoid body water escaping through the mouth, and works to keep the body hydrated longer.

Those working outdoors should be able to recognize the symptoms of heat-related illnesses and heat emergencies. These include the previously-covered health threats of moderate or severe sunburn, heat cramps, heat rash, heat exhaustion, and heat strokes. It's always a good idea to either learn or know first aid measures—or at least what to do should any of these particular threats occur. For each particular heat-related affliction (described on pages 19-21) that might occur during extremely hot weather, there are particular recommended courses of action one can take to help mitigate the symptoms of each condition.

Sunburn

The best single measure against the possibility of sunburn is applying *sunscreen* to the skin before exposure to the sun, especially in hot weather. Sunscreens are lotion-based products that, when applied to the skin, offers a great measure of protection against the harmful effects of the sun's UVA and UVB rays. The effectiveness of sunscreens is dependent upon its "SPF" (Sun-Protection Factor), the way by which these products are measured in terms of their ability to counter the harmful effects extended exposure to the sun. The effectiveness of sunscreens is also based on the skin type of those undergoing exposure; skin type affects how easily one sunburns. Those with darker-skin complexions such as African-Americans have a very low (but not zero) probability of experiencing sunburns, even without protection. On the other hand, those with very fair skin types, such as redheads will sunburn very easily—with varying degrees of susceptibility for those with skin types in between the two extremes.

It should be noted that a sunscreen's SPF is not a measure of the amount of protection per se. What SPF indicates is how long it will take for UVA & UVB rays to begin turning the skin red while wearing sunscreen compared to how long it would without protection (on average, it takes approximately 20 minutes of unprotected exposure to the sun's UV rays to begin burning the skin). As an example, someone using a sunscreen with an SPF of 15 will take 15 times longer for the skin to redden than without the sunscreen.   An SPF 15 sunscreen screens 93% of the sun's UVB rays; SPF 30 protects against 97%; and SPF 50, 98%. Most medical professionals agree that sunscreens with an SPF of 15 or higher are necessary for adequate protection (some medical professionals argue that using sunscreens with an SPF of 30 is better, though higher SPFs are believed to offer no greater amount of protection against sunburn, except in cases of many hours of exposure). And sunscreens should be—regardless of the degree of protection offered—reapplied every couple of hours, as they can be washed away as the skin begins to perspire in hot weather.

Hours in the Sun	Very Fair Never tans, always burns	Fair Tans slowly, burns easily	Light Usually burns fast	Medium Burns minimally	Dark Rarely burns
1	SPF 20	SPF 20	SPF 0-10	SPF 0-10	
2	SPF 30	SPF 30	SPF 30	SPF 20	SPF 0-10
3	SPF 40	SPF 30	SPF 30	SPF 20	
4	SPF 40	SPF 40		SPF 30	SPF 20
5	SPF 50	SPF 50	SPF 40		

A chart indicating the recommended level of SPF needed for optimum protection against the harmful effects of the sun's UVA and UVB rays, based on skin types and expected hours of exposure.

In addition to wearing sunscreens, those expecting hot weather exposure need to consider other ways to prevent sunburn to exposed areas of the body, including wearing a lip balm in conjunction with sunscreens. Consider avoiding direct sunlight exposure when possible, particularly between the hours of 10am and 3pm when the sun's light are the most intense. If staying indoors is not possible, drinking plenty of water before venturing outside is highly recommended. This is because sunburns are known to actually draw fluids to the surface of the skin, away from other parts of the body (for this reason, it is best to not only drink plenty of water during hot weather periods, but to rehydrate with plenty of fluids often).

The No-Nonsense Guide To Heat Wave, Drought, & Hot Weather Safety

When outside, the proper type clothing one chooses to wear can offer a great (although not an absolute) measure of protection against harmful sun rays. Comfortable long-sleeved shirts, along with pants composed of tightly woven fabrics are the best choices when possible. It is also recommended that a wide-brimmed model of hat/headwear be worn; such articles provide their own shade and help keep the head cooler. Sunglasses are also advisable, especially if they are designed to block the majority of UVA and UVB rays.

In the event that sunburn has taken place, it is important to begin treating it in order to expedite the skin's healing process There are several steps one can take to aid the healing of the affected skin.

- Taking a cool shower or bath can lower the temperature of the affected skin. Additionally, covering the affected part(s) of the body with a clean wet, cool towel will have the same effect. The latter option can be done for 10-15 minutes each day until the skin starts to become noticeably normalized in color and appearance.
- Moisturizers may be applied to the affected skin and body to help soothe any pain and/or burning sensations caused by the sunburn. Lotions that contain aloe vera are a particularly good choice as a soothing agent. Hydrocortisone creams can also be applied to sunburned skin, especially skin that is blistering to reduce inflammation. Avoid the use of products which contain the ingredients *benzocaine* or *lidocaine.* These can cause allergy and irritate the skin in some individuals, and actually make the burn worse. Also, avoid the use of petroleum jelly or similar petroleum-based applications (petroleum-based products can trap the heat of sunburn within the skin, which may irritate and cause more pain in the affected skin).
- Blisters can also be covered with dry bandages in order to help prevent infection (blistered skin is an indication of a more severe second-degree sunburn that may require a doctor's attention if it gets worse).
- It might be advisable to purchase over-the-counter medicines, such as ibuprofen or acetaminophen to help relieve any pain from sunburn (avoid giving for aspirin for pain to children).
- Loose clothing made of a cotton-based material should be worn to over sunburned skin to protect it as it heals. In dressing to prevent sunburn, tightly-woven fabrics work best (when the fabric is held up to a bright light, you shouldn't see any light coming through.
- In severe sunburn cases (such as those involving third-degree sunburns), seek medical attention from a qualified physician or dermatologist.

Heat Cramps

Although heat cramps typically run their own course within 24 hours of the initial onset of cramping, there are self-treatments that may help ease the symptoms, or speed up the process of ending cramps.

- All physical activity should be stopped.
- Individuals suspecting that they may be experiencing heat cramps should rest in a cool environment and drink fluids—preferably mixed with salt—in order to replace lost minerals. Commercial sports drinks may also provide an adequate source of dietary salt. However, salt tablets by themselves should not be used, as they can upset the stomach upset. Furthermore, salt tablets don't adequately replace fluid lost through sweating.

• If possible, cramping muscles should be gently stretched to help relax them. Heat cramps usually involve muscles that are fatigued by heavy work, such as calves, thighs, and shoulders
• Muscle pain may be treated with over-the-counter pain-relievers such as those containing ibuprofen.

Despite the after-the-fact treatments, prevention is still the best overall treatment for heat cramps. While admittedly not always possible, efforts should be made to avoid working and/or exercising in the heat of the day, especially in hot weather. If physically-demanding activity in the heat can't be avoided, it might become necessary to try to slowly allow oneself to become acclimated to the high temperatures first. Keep drinks nearby, and rehydrate often. If the activity is expected to lasts for an extended period of time, consider using commercial sports drinks (not energy drinks). This is especially true if significant sweating occurs and salt and other vital minerals are lost through sweat. Finally, frequent breaks should also be indulged to avoid tiring out the muscles entirely, and to allow an easy pacing on one's activities.

Heat Exhaustion

In suspected cases of heat exhaustion, it is vitally important to begin the process of helping the body cool down. Doing so also prevents the condition itself from advancing into the more severe and life-threatening condition of heat stroke (see below). Among the important steps to take to lessen heat exhaustion are:

• Individuals suspected of experiencing heat exhaustion should be relocated to a cooler environment, preferably an air-conditioned indoor location. If such an environment is not available, the affected person should be moved out of direct sun, and into a shady area.
• Those suspected of suffering from heat exhaustion should lie down and elevate their legs and feet slightly. Clothing—which will probably be sweat-soaked—should be loosened or removed.
• The ailing individual should drink cool water or other fluids that could restore hydration. The use of caffeine-based products (such as soda) should be avoided.[23]
• A water-soaked towel can be applied to the skin of the affected individual to assist in cooling the body. A cool shower or bath can be used as a substitute for cold-compress applications.
• The afflicted individual should be monitored carefully. If the condition deteriorates or continues longer than 30-minutes after cool measures have been undertaken, medical assistance should be summoned right away (call 911 in most North American locations and 112 in European locations). Heat exhaustion can quickly become heatstroke, especially if fainting, confusion or seizures occur. Also, a persistent fever of 104 F (40 C) or greater is an indication of a worsening condition.

As with most illnesses, particularly heat-related ones, being proactive in preventing the threat of heat exhaustion is the best form of treatment. If working or exercising in the heat is optional, consider postponing such activities until later in the day, when temperatures cool. Staying inside in a cool (e.g.,

---

[23] Caffeine is diuretic, which causes frequent urination. With regard to dehydration, drinking caffeinated drinks may actually cause the loss of more bodily fluids, not less.

air-conditioned) setting during the hottest period of the day is the best course of action, when possible. Other precautions that can help stave off the threat of this particular heat-related illness include:

.
- Drinking fluids during exercise helps improve heart function, maintain kidney function, and lower the body's core temperature. Dehydration can stress the heart and reduce the kidneys' ability to maintain the correct balance of electrolytes (charged elements—such as potassium, sodium, phosphorous, and chloride—which are essential for the normal function of every cell in the body). Alcohol-based beverages, like caffeine-based ones, should be avoided. Water, sports drinks, and natural fruit juices are the preferred choices of hydration.
- Drink 2 cups of water 30 minutes before exercising and drink 1 cup of water every 20 minutes.
- Cool baths both before and after strenuous activities is a sensible precaution to help keep the skin cool.
- Loose, lightweight clothing should be worn, as opposed clothing composed of heavier fabrics.
- Physically-intense activity should be paced. Those who exercise or work regularly in hot weather should allow their bodies to adjust to hot conditions, and take frequent breaks while active.

Heat Stroke

Heat stroke can cause damage to the brain as well as other internal organs, resulting in death if not treated in a timely manner. Common symptoms include nausea, seizures, confusion, disorientation, and sometimes loss of consciousness...or the affected person may slip into a coma. Other symptoms may include:

- An extremely high body temperature (above 103 F, as measured orally by a thermometer)
- Skin that turns red in color that is often hot (and dry) to the touch (by this point, sweating has stopped entirely)
- A rapid, strong pulse
- A particularly throbbing (intense) headache
- Rapid, shallow breathing
- Behavioral changes such as confusion, disorientation, or staggering
- Dizziness, light-headedness
- Muscle weakness or cramps

Although heat stroke mainly affects people over age 50 (the elderly are at particular high-risk), it can also occur in young, relatively healthy athletes. Heat stroke almost, always requires emergency medical attention, therefore a call to 911 (112) is imperative to ensure timely medical intervention—and prevent death (or permanent disability).

While waiting for the paramedics to arrive, cooling measures and first-aid should begin immediately. The affected person should be relocated to an air-conditioned environment (or a cooler, shady area if outdoors). Unnecessary clothing should be removed immediately. Begin additional measures restore the body's core temperature should be initiated immediately:

- Fan air over the patient while applying a cold compress (i.e., towel soaked in cold water) to the skin of

the affected person. Hosing the victim off with a garden hose or simply immersing him/her in a tub of cool water or a shower will also help cool the skin.
- Apply ice packs to the patient's armpits, groin, neck, and back (because these areas of the body are rich with blood vessels closer to the surface of the skin. Cooling these areas may reduce body temperature quicker).
- Continue to monitor body temperature, and continue cooling efforts until the body temperature drops to 101-102 F.
- Oftentimes, someone suffering a heat stroke will begin experiencing involuntary and uncontrollable muscle will twitches (spasms). In this instance, efforts should be made to keep the victim injuring himself. Avoid the urge to place any object in the victim's mouth in the event of seizures. Also, refrain from serving the victim any fluids. If there is vomiting, make sure the airway remains open by turning the victim on his or her side.
- Avoid giving the victim alcohol or caffeine-based drinks.
- If emergency medical personnel are delayed, call the hospital emergency room for further instructions.

As with all heat-related illnesses, prevention is the best form of treatment; taking measures to ensure that health does not deteriorate in hot weather, particularly during heat waves. During hot weather, it is imperative to protect oneself by taking measures to literally stay cool and use common sense. The following tips are important:

- Drinking plenty of cool liquids at intermittent periods should be a priority practice—regardless of one's activity level. Very cold beverages should be avoided since they can cause cramping of the stomach, as should alcoholic drinks. During heavy exercise or strenuous activity in hot weather, it is advisable to drink at least 2-4 glasses (.48 - .95 liters) of cool fluids each hour. However, it may be necessary to drink more liquid than one's thirst indicates, as dehydration is a subtle process, and many people may not know they are losing more fluids than is safe...until it is too late. This is especially true for people 65 years of age and older who often have a decreased ability to respond to external temperature changes.
- In addition to cool fluids, it is important to maintain salt and other vital mineral levels in the body during hot weather (as heavy sweating removes salt and minerals from the body). The easiest and safest way to replace salt and minerals is through diet and drinking (e.g., fruit juices or sports beverages). In the event that an individual is on a physician-directed low-salt/sodium diet, it is advisable to contact a medical professional before using a sports drink or altering one's diet for hot weather.
- Appropriate clothing and SPF-level sunscreen should be worn for the environment. Lightweight, light-colored, loose-fitting clothing is best. Apply sunscreen 30 minutes before going outdoors and reapply every 2 hours, of as instructed on the directions.
- Individuals expecting to perform activities in hot weather should be prepared to pace themselves, starting slowly and gradually picking up the pace is the best course of action. Frequent breaks during work and/or exercise should be observed. If an increase in heart rate or pulse, lightheadedness, confusion becomes noticeable, or shortness of breath is observed, all activity should be stopped

immediately. Anyone experiencing these changes, particularly in hot weather should relocate to a cooler or shaded and seek rest. Plan any strenuous activities until the cooler hours of the day.

- Staying indoors in an air-conditioned area during extremely hot weather is the most efficient way to avoid threats associated with the heat. In the event that a residence isn't equipped with a cooling unit of any kind, many public venues *are* cooled with central-air. Visiting one of these venues in the form of a shopping mall or public library for a few hours is an effective alternative. Additionally, many large and medium-sized cities have a policy of opening "cooling centers" [24] to assist with keeping those who don't have access to air-conditioning cool. Electric fans may be useful in the absence of air-conditioning, but should not be relied upon as a primary source for relief, particularly during a heat wave. In most cases, fans will provide very little comfort when the temperatures reach the mid to high 90°F (32°C) threshold—nor will fans prevent potential heat-related illness at that point. It is also a good idea to avoid using stoves and ovens during the heat of the day; postpone their use until the cooler hours of the day.

- It is a good idea to establish a "well-bring check" among one's circle of family and acquaintances, particularly among those who suffer from a chronic illness and the elderly. Arrange for someone to call and/or visit anyone who might bet at particular risk for heat-related illnesses, particularly in hot weather. Heat-induced illness can cause a person to become confused or lose consciousness. In such an instance, venerable individuals may not be able to easily contact someone for assistance, so checking in on such individuals becomes all the more important. Those who might be under consideration for well-being checks are:
  - Infants and children up to four years of age
  - People 65 years of age or older
  - People who are overweight
  - People who are ill or on certain medications

- Never underestimate the power of common sense thinking. Eating hot foods and heavy meals during hot weather adds heat to already warm bodies; they should be avoided. Infants, children, or pets should NEVER left alone in parked vehicles, even if only for 5 minutes. It simply doesn't take long in

Category	Classification	Heat Index/Apparent Temperature	General Affect on People in High Risk Groups
I	Extremely Hot	130°F or Higher (54°C or Higher)	Heat/Sunstroke HIGHLY LIKELY with continued exposure
II	Very Hot	105°F - 130°F (41°C - 54°C)	Sunstroke, heat cramps, or heat exhaustion LIKELY, and heat stroke POSSIBLE with prolonged exposure and/or physical activity
III	Hot	90°F - 105°F (32°C - 41°C)	Sunstroke, heat cramps, or heat exhaustion POSSIBLE with prolonged exposure and/or physical activity
IV	Very Warm	80°F - 90°F (27°C - 32°C)	Fatigue POSSIBLE with prolonged exposure and/or physical activity

[24] Cooling centers are temporarily-established, air-conditioned public venues set up by local authorities to deal with the potential health effects of a heat wave. These centers are usually situated at several established locations throughout a city such as public libraries. Low-income and the elderly residents are particularly encouraged to make use of these centers during hot weather and heat waves. Those who feel that they may have need for such facilities should contact their local health department in order locate any heat-relief shelters in their area.

hot weather for the interior of a vehicle parked in the sun to become unbearably hot. Infants and young children especially should be dressed in cool, loose clothing. Additionally, their heads and faces should be covered, and/or protected with sunscreen made especially for children. Sun exposure should be limited during the mid-day hours, especially in open fields and beaches—areas of potential severe exposure. Ensure that infants and children drink adequate amounts of liquids.

Finally, pets should have access to plenty of fresh water; leave the water in a shady area. In the more serious cases of heat exhaustion and heat stroke, **always** call emergency services immediately (911).

Common Sense Rules

Just as in most situations involving an element of danger, a level of common sense can be applied to remaining safe in extremely hot weather. The first common sense rule is to watch for signs of heat stress and/or heat-related illnesses in family members and close acquaintances. This applies particularly to those individuals who might be especially vulnerable to [the] high levels of heat and humidity. Elderly people, young children, and those who are sick or overweight are more likely to become victims of extreme heat. It's a good practice to check in on elderly and/ or sick neighbors who are known to live alone. If any such individuals are known not have air-conditioning, local emergency services might be able to assist them. But it is always better to perform a well-being check personally to ensure their safety.

Never leave children or family pets alone in a closed vehicle. This may seemingly go without saying, but every year in the U.S., an average of 38 children die each year from being left unattended in closed vehicles.[25] Anyone who observes a child in such a situation should contact 911 immediately. A closed automobile on a summer day, especially an extremely hot day, can become a virtual oven in as little as 15 minutes.

Avoid using salt tablets unless directed to do so by a physician. Salt causes the body to retain fluids, resulting in swelling. Salt also affects areas of the body that help it sweat. This is what keeps us cool on hot days. Individual on salt-restrictive diets should check with a physician before increasing salt intake.

In the event of a heat emergency, take measures to keep the victim cool until help arrives (provide shade and a cool bath to help lower the body temperature of any victim of a serious heat emergency). Key symptoms of a heat emergency to watch for include:

- Rapid breathing
- Lack of sweating
- Pale, hot, and/or red skin
- High temperature/fever
- Twitching muscles
- Possible vomiting
- Fainting or unconsciousness

---

[25] "Heatstroke Deaths of Children in Vehicles," Department of Meteorology & Climate Science, San Jose State University. http://www.ggweather.com/heat/

The No-Nonsense Guide To Heat Wave, Drought, & Hot Weather Safety

Drought

Before a Drought

   As droughts are generally difficult to predict, the most effective means of preparation is to simply consider that droughts can strike any place—outside of deserts, tropical rain forests, or the earth's Polar Regions—where rain normally falls. Taking these factors into consideration, a somewhat effective strategy to keep abreast of the potential for a drought is to monitor long-term weather forecasts. Federal departments n charge of monitoring meteorological conditions in many countries will post these forecasts online. Additionally, television news stations will occasionally broadcasts 30-day weather outlooks for both particular regions—based on computer models—as well as for an entire country. It might be noteworthy from time to time to take note of how much rain one's immediate area has received during the past month and/or year (television news stations will broadcast this statistic, usually daily). Areas that normally experience comparatively low-levels of precipitation from year to year are at a particular risk for droughts. For those residing in such areas during the time of drought, the twin priorities of conserving water, and maximizing the limited available water becomes of paramount importance.

In-Home Preparations
   In conserving water, perhaps the simplest action one can perform is purchase bottled water. The water purchased should be tightly sealed and stored in a cool location, away from direct sunlight. Because water—especially sealed –can be kept for an extended period of time, it does not have to be thrown out and replaced (most experts believe bottled water has an indefinite self-life).
   Efforts to avoid the potential waste of water should be undertaken as dry weather approaches. And one of the most significant wasters of water is leaks, be those that occur directly from pipes or from faucets in and around a home or dwelling. One way to check for leaks is to locate a building's water meter, which can be mounted either inside or outside—depending on the type of dwelling (commercial, government, or residential). Once the meter is located, make a note of the current readings (if digital) or dial(s) setting (if analogue), and then shut off all faucets and the entire building and avoid using water for about a 2-hour period. If the reading on the meter has changed at all during that two-hour shut-off period, then there is likely a water leak occurring somewhere in inside.
   Indoor plumbing should be visually inspected for any possible leaks, especially faucets. Leaky faucets should be repaired by replacing worn washers, while leaky pipes may require the services of a licensed plumber or other professional repairperson. A single drop of water per second leak can result in an accumulated loss of about 2,700 gallons (10,220 liters) of water in a single year, from a single household. Another option is to fit faucets and shower nozzles with water flow restrictors. As their name implies, these devices limit the amount of water that comes from a tap, which saves the amount of water used.
   In the bathroom, toilets are the single biggest user of water. The amount of water used can be reduced by purchasing a low-volume toilet that uses less than half the water of older model toilets. In many newer homes, these low water-use toilets are standard fixtures. And in many areas in the U.S., low-volume units are required by law.

Outdoor Preparations

Just as making relatively minor changes to indoor plumbing and water-use habits can help conserve the amount of water used during a water shortage, there are measures one can apply outside a home or building to further reduce the strains on regional water supplies before they become affected by drought. This may involve employing strategies that help avoid using household water supplies for all but the most important needs, while making use of whatever water becomes available in the course of normal daily activities. A key avenue to accomplish this is to gather and use rainwater (when it *does* rain. It should be noted that droughts are not necessarily the absence of rain, but less than normal rainfall).

It may be worth the expense to purchase a rain barrel or some type of open container capable of collecting/capturing rainwater. And the best way to maximize these rainwater collectors is to place them at the base of each downspout around a home or dwelling. Collecting and using rainwater can save homeowners upwards of an estimated 1,300 gallons (4,921 liters) of water annually. What's more, rainwater is often free of many of the same potentially harmful chemicals such as chlorine, impure calcium deposits, found in municipal water supplies. This collected rainwater can be used for purposes that are less vital than say, washing or drinking. Rainwater gathered in this way could be—for example—diverted to create an irrigation system to water small crops (or as water for animals/pets).

For those whose livelihoods depend primarily on weather conditions such as those whose businesses rely a great deal on both the weather and the outdoor use of land, additional preparations may be required to protect against economic losses. For ranchers, specialty planters, and subsistence/production farmers, this may include the need to secure *crop insurance*. Crop insurance is a type of specialty insurance that farmers and other such self-employed individuals purchase to protect against their plants, crops and marketable commodities against loss due to natural disasters. [26]

For the most part, crop insurance may be purchased in one of two different types:

- Crop-yield Insurance is generally available from private insurers, with some aspects of it being subsidized by the federal government in the U.S. (in other countries such as France, crop-yield insurance may be either similarly purchased from private insurance companies). This particular class of insurance can be underwritten to cover a particular type of natural disaster (e.g., hail), or multiple risk perils (such as plant diseases, drought, or other types of disasters) under the option of multi-peril crop insurance (MPCI) policy. MPCI coverage is usually offered by a government insurer, with premiums (monthly payments that cover the cost of the insurance policy) partially subsidized by the Federal Crop Insurance Corporation under the United States Department of Agriculture (and likewise in Canada by the departments within the federal and provincial governments).

---

[26] For cattle ranchers, a vocation that is just as dependent plants (for animal food/feed) on plants and the weather as farmers, the option of *livestock insurance* may be substituted for crop insurance to protect against any negative economic effects of drought. To obtain basic information on livestock insurance (in the U.S.), the United States Department of Agriculture (USDA) offers a primer on its website (http://www.usda.gov/wps/portal/usda/usdahome?navid=CROP_LIVESTOCK_INSUR).

- <u>Crop-revenue insurance</u> is a type of insurance which offers protection against economic losses that affect the expected regular income from the sale of commodities (that may have been damaged from disasters such as droughts). This is to say that crop-revenue—as its name implies—protects farmers and other such self-employed individuals against crop-revenue losses. This type of insurance policy pays a monetary compensation for crop losses if there is a deficit between the price of the actual crop yield and the cash settlement price the insured is offered based on projections in the crop commodities' futures market. In the case of drought, crop-revenue insurance will cover income losses that might occur if drought lowers the amount expected from the sale of crops damaged in said drought. In the United States, the program is called Crop Revenue Coverage.[27]

When considering the purchase of crop insurance each prospective purchaser makes three decisions: coverage level (based on the total projected value of the marketable commodity), crop insurance type, and unit type (type of crop/commodity). Each of these decisions impacts the calculation of payments in the event of losses from disasters like drought. It is for this reason that many insurers offer individualized insurance plans, which are based on [the] production of marketable commodities, and the revenue history of sales of said commodity.

During A Drought

Indoors

The bathroom, particularly the toilet is a primary source of water usage—and savings—in preparing the home for drought situations. Other than the obvious human waste, other sorts of refuse that one may be tempted to throw into the toilet should be thrown instead into the trash. Restricting flushing to bodily waste only saves a lot of water by reducing unnecessary flushing. Another strategy to conserve water through toilet usage is to consider placing an item such as a plastic container (or similar item) in the tank of the toilet in order to displace the water inside. Displacing the water in the tank serves to cut down on the amount of water needed to flush.[28]

Other bathroom-related water-saving strategies include limiting showers to 5-6 minutes to use less water. The water should be turned on to get wet, turned off to lather up, and finally turned back on in order to rinse off. The same pattern can be used to wash hair. A bucket or other type of container can be used to catch excess water for other uses.[29] Also, constantly running the water when shaving and/or brushing teeth should be avoided. A better option is to run the water *only* when rising off either a razor

---

[27] Crop-revenue insurance covers the decline in price that occurs during the crop's growing season. It does not cover declines that may occur from one growing season to another. Additionally, the USDA administers a program that assist non-insured agricultural commodities producers (http://www.fsa.usda.gov/FSA/webapp?area=home&subject=diap&topic=nap).

[28] When installing a water displacement item in the toilet tank, the item should be placed in such a manner as to not interfere with moving mechanical/operating parts of the toilet itself.

[29] Consider other uses for water before pouring it down the drain. Dishwater water could be used, for example, to water indoor houseplants or gardens. And drained cooking water could be allowed to cool off and given to house pets.

or toothbrush...just long enough for each intermittent rise. Another option is to fill a large cup up with water and use it to rinse each item after using it.

The kitchen is another prime area of the home to consider saving water. The water amounts used for washing dishes, for example can be cut by purchasing and filling 2 water open water containers (one with soapy water, and the other with clear water containing a small amount of a disinfectant such as bleach) and hand-washing dishes instead of using an automatic dishwasher (with the soapy water used for washing dishes, and the clear water used for rinsing them). However, if using an automatic dishwasher is more practical, it should operated only when it is fully loaded with dishes and eating utensils. Because an automatic dishwasher can use up toward 14 gallons (53 liters) of water in a single cycle, a "light wash" or similar water-saving setting should be used during water-shortages. And avoid rinsing dishes before placing them in the dishwasher (most automatic dishwashers can clean dirty dishes very enough so that they do not have to be pre-rinsed. Large fragments of food can be removed manually and thrown out).

In preparing food, water usage can be curtailed...with a minimal loss of sanitation. One way to save water as it pertains to food is to avoid running warm/hot water to thaw out meat or other frozen foods. Alternatives such as allowing food to sit out at room temperature for approximately 2 hours prior to preparation can work just as well. Another way to defrost frozen food without water is to use the defrost setting on an available microwave. When it comes to washing certain foods such as vegetables, using a bowl or pan filled with water saves more money than cleaning with running water from a faucet (again, the used water from the bowl can be reused for other purposes).

Finally, when washing clothes, changing laundry habits can also save water. One way is to wash clothes fewer times than one would in a period with normal precipitation and water availability. Also, washing laundry should only be done so when there is a full load of clothes; washing a small amount of clothing simply waste more water than is necessary. Washing in cold or warm water saves heated water for times when its need is more crucial (it's also more cost-efficient to use cooler water temperatures). And during times when only a single article of clothing—or maybe 1 or 2 items—need to be washed, consider hand washing in a tub of water, so as not to have to wait until a full wash load is available.

Outdoors

A variation of the water collection strategy can be used to provide water for individual plants. Unused plastic containers (such as milk jugs or plastic bottles) could be used to collect rainwater or filled with small amounts of tap water, and placed in close proximity to plants. Poke small holes into these containers with a pin or ice pick and allow the water to saturate plant's root system; water plants only in the morning. And in areas where groundwater is known to exist, wells could be dug in order to tap into underground sources of water. For those already using wells as their primary source for water, it is a good practice to periodically check water pumps for proper functioning (if an automatic pump turns on and off while water is not being used, this is an indication of a leak somewhere in the home). For well-water users, the same suggestions for water conservation apply.

As maintaining the vitality of garden plants and/or the upkeep a lawn is important for many, there are steps one can take that would both curtail unnecessary water usage as well as maintain these interests. If one *must* resort to using the regular water supply to maintain lawns and/or gardens, consider implementing strategies that make use of lesser amounts of water. Avoid over-watering lawns and water only when needed. In the event of rain, it will not be necessary to water lawns and plants. A heavy rain eliminates the need for watering for up to two weeks. Most of the year, lawns only need one inch of water per week. During periods without rain, lawn and hose sprinklers should be positioned so as to avoid spraying and wasting water on areas around a home, such as a sidewalk or patio. The timing of automatic sprinklers should be adjusted to operate in smaller time intervals.[30] This practice of less time and watering can be applied also to those who hand-water their lawns. When lawns require watering, it should be done so early in the morning or later in the evening, when temperatures are cooler. Cooler temperatures take advantage of less evaporation of whatever water is present.

Another alternative to sprinkler- and hand-watering plants and/or lawns is water-efficient irrigation. One such system, *drip irrigation*, is a highly efficient way to water. A drip irrigation system is constructed in such a way so as to deliver water directly to the root zone of a plant, where it seeps slowly into the soil one crop at a time. Very little water is lost through surface runoff or evaporation. What makes this particular system of irrigation efficient is that is that it forces water directly on the particular plants and vegetation that needs it, and not on nearby weeds that may choke off the important plant's roots. Like other such water-saving alternative methods of watering plants, targeted irrigation systems like drip irrigation can use anywhere from 30 to 50% less water than watering by hand or with a sprinkler system. What's more, this alternative system of watering important plants can work for small-scale farms (and with some modification, such a system can be applied to suit the needs of larger farmers).

A graphic depicting a drip-irrigation-type setup for small trees. The alternative system is equally effective for small gardens and shrubbery.

Whether those affected by drought be homeowners concerned about prized plants, subsistence farmers who grow their own food supplies, or commercial producers who produce food-plants to sell in the market place, the goals and methods of saving water applies. Moreover, there are several other water-saving practices that anyone with similar concerns can implement water-management strategies to help conserve limited water during drought conditions. The first of these strategies is the most basic; the practical and careful monitoring of weather forecasts in order to avoid under- or overwatering crops and plants. Any attempts to keep lawns, plants, and/or crops alive and (comparatively) healthy during lean-water times should be adjusted to coincide with knowing how much moisture soil and plants

---

[30] And avoid leaving sprinklers unattended. A garden hose can discharge upwards of 600 gallons (2,271 liters) or more in only a few hours.

contain at any given time during this period. Establishing a regular irrigation/watering schedule that takes into account these factors will maximize the use of limited water—given any local and/or regional restrictions—during prolonged dry weather periods.

Other strategies—some involving being proactive—can be just as effective in mitigating the use of water during periods of drought. Some of these strategies include:

- Growing drought-tolerant crops (or planting drought-resistant plants). Those concerned with protecting prized (or valuable) plants and crops during periods of drought can sow plant species that are appropriate to a regions particular climate. Plants which are native to arid regions (i.e., regions that are accustomed to little or no precipitation) are naturally drought-tolerant. Such plants can be planted in lieu of high-maintenance turf grasses. There are several brands and types of drought-resistance grasses that are available commercially. Also, there are many drought-resistance crops that one can consider planting that can be equally as profitable, dependent upon given markets and demands.

- "Dry Farming" is a type of farming/planting practice that is based on plant production during dry weather. This technique utilizes residual moisture in the soil from previous saturation (such a previous rains or morning dew/condensation). Dry farming works to conserve soil moisture during long dry periods primarily through a specialized method of tilling the soil, surface protection, and the use of drought-resistant plant/crop types.

- Introducing organic materials into the soil can aid overall in conserving water. The use of *compost* (decomposed natural/organic matter used as fertilizer) in the soil of prized plants/crops can help improve the soil's ability to conserve moisture. Organic *mulches* (material spread on top of the soil to conserve moisture) such as those made from straw or wood chips can be spread around plants to further increase the soil's ability to retain water. What's more, organic mulches will eventually break down into compost, which will help plants retain moisture (as well as provide as additional source of fertilizer).

In addition to these semi-proactive strategies, it might be worth considering employing landscaping techniques that require less watering rationing during drought situations. Smaller areas of a yard can actually be used for grass and plants, reducing the overall areas of a yard/lawn that needs to be maintained (and watered). Moreover, less fertilizer can be used on lawns. Over-fertilizing a lawn/land area increases the need for water—thus less fertilizers means less watering. Also, there are lawn fertilizers on the market that contain slow-release, water-insoluble forms of nitrogen. Lawns fertilized by this particular alternative can go longer between watering.

When it becomes necessary to cut and/or trim lawns, how this is done can also potentially affect water usage. To cut down on the need for more watering, something as simple as adjusting the blade height of a lawn mower can impact how a law retains water. If the blade of a mower is adjusted to at

In the graphic above, notice the comparative root systems of the cut grass depictions. The higher-cut grass on the right has an expanded root system that is able to maintain greater amounts of moisture...and therefore require less watering

least 3inches (7.6 centimeters) or to its highest level, this would encourages grass roots to grow deeper, resulting in creating more potential shade for a lawn's root system. And this would help the soil retain more moisture.

Planting alternatives to traditional grass lawns is another option that can save the use of water outdoors. Putting a layer of mulch around trees and plants can help to reduce the evaporation of moisture, while keeping the surrounding soil cool. Organic mulch also improves the soil by helping to fertilize it, while helping to prevent the growth of plant-choking weeds.

Finally, for those who insist on washing their vehicles during a drought, the best option is to cut back on the number of times a vehicle was washed. Waiting longer between washings saves water. But if personal expense is not an issue, vehicles can be washed at a commercial car wash—preferably one where recycled water is used. If washing a vehicle at home, it is best to use a shut-off nozzle that can be adjusted down to a fine spray setting on a watering hose. Also, parking a vehicle on the grass while washing prevents wasting water, as the grass will be watered as the same time.

Local Ordinances

During severe droughts, many local and regional municipalities may institute legal restrictions placed on the use of water. These ordinances are intended to compel—by force of law—residents of a drought-affected area to curb their use of water by outlining when, and under what particular conditions water from a common source (such as a reservoir) may be used. In most cases, restrictions placed on water use tend to be implemented in "stages." Although the particular restrictions within a particular "stage" varies from municipality to municipality, most follow a general guideline of restrictions based on the severity of water depletion related to drought conditions.[31] For example, in

---

[31] The numbers of stages that constitute water restrictions also vary from municipality to municipality.

many areas of the U.S., town, city, and even county governments may mandate that watering lawns or washing cars may only be performed during certain hours of the day, or on certain days of the week when a municipality institutes "stage one water restrictions." During particularly extreme drought conditions, such as those Australia often experiences, more rigid restrictions may be placed on the use

	Water Supply Level	Stage 1 Normal	Stage 2 Moderate	Stage 3 Acute	Stage 4 Severe
	Effective Dates:	May 1 – Sept 30			
RESIDENTIAL	Sprinkling of lawns, trees, shrubs, flowers or vegetables			Not allowed	Not allowed
	Even addresses	Tues, Thurs, Sun 7-9 am and 7-9 pm	Thurs, Sun 7-9 am		
	Odd addresses	Mon, Wed, Sat 7-9 am and 7-9 pm	Wed, Sat 7-9 am		
	Unestablished new lawns	By permit only, must be displayed on lawn.	As per existing permit. No new permits issued.	Not allowed	Not allowed
	Hand watering trees, shrubs, flowers and vegetables	OK at any time, ONLY with spray-trigger nozzle.	OK at any time, ONLY with spray-trigger nozzle.	By hand-held container ONLY	Not allowed
	Washing vehicles or boats	ONLY with spray-trigger nozzle	ONLY with spray-trigger nozzle	Not allowed	Not allowed
	Hosing of sidewalks and driveways, windows or exterior building surfaces	ONLY with spray-trigger nozzle or pressure washer	Not allowed except to pressure wash surfaces to prep for paint, etc., or as required by law for safety.	Not allowed	Not allowed
	Filling swimming pools, spas, garden ponds, decorative fountains	OK	OK	Not allowed	Not allowed
NON-RESIDENTIAL	Sprinkling of lawns, trees, shrubs, flowers or vegetables	Same as for Residential	Same as for Residential	Same as for Residential	Not allowed
	Commercial Operations	No restrictions	No restrictions	Essential uses only. Will be contacted to cut back on use.	Not allowed
PUBLIC	Sprinkling of landscaped areas, ornamental gardens	Same as Residential schedule	Same as Residential schedule	Not allowed	Not allowed
	Sprinkling of sports fields, maintaining public swimming pools, water parks	Separate schedule	Separate schedule	Not allowed	Not allowed

A chart outlining the stages and requirements of each state of water restrictions from the Canadian province of British Columbia. Note how the restrictions for each state become more rigid, depending on the severity of the drought conditions and common water availability.

of water in latter stages. In October of 2007, the town council of Kingaroy initiated "stage 7" water restrictions, which prohibited all outdoor use of water without a legal permit—except in cases of fires.

Water restrictions are not limited to local "stage" water restrictions. During a multi-year drought that stretched into 2014, the state of California experienced so little rainfall that the state government instituted state-wide water –use restrictions. These restrictions prohibited, among other infractions, any outdoor watering that causes runoff, the use of a watering hose without a shutoff nozzle, applying water to hard surfaces like sidewalks or driveways, and using water in fountains and other decorative yard features.

Keep in mind that during a drought, officials may recommend (and sometimes require) water restriction measures that include such procedures as watering lawns and washing cars on odd or even days of the week, at night, or on weekends. When such water restrictions are put into effect, they are done so for a simple reason; to maintain water availability during periods of low rainfall and low water levels in common water sources. It is important that these rules be followed. Anyone who is unaware of which particular water restrictions might be in place in their area(s) during drought conditions should check with their local authorities or water utility for information in that regard.

After A Heat Wave

Because heat waves tend to be of a shorter duration than droughts, their environmental effects tend to be less extensive. Still, it is always better to err on the side of caution when temperatures return to normal levels. First and foremost, continue to monitor any victims of serious heat-related illnesses, particularly those who might have suffered heat exhaustion and heat stroke. There is always a chance that medical complications may result from any serious conditions, and might require further medical treatment.

The widespread use of power-draining air conditioners will have dropped radically as temperatures return to normal. This means that there will be less stress placed on local and regional power grids. In most cases, it will likely be safe to resume normal electric appliance usage. However, it may be necessary to resume energy-saving practices should extreme temperatures return; this happens often in summers where temperatures consistently range higher than normal.

On some occasions, intense heat waves may cause damage to dwellings or aspects of a region's infrastructure. In such cases, repairs should begin as soon as weather conditions allow. In the case of damage to electrical power grids, this may mean the inconvenience of being without power for as long as a day or two. A properly-prepared and stocked "emergency disaster kit" would address such a contingency. Also when driving, be aware of the possibility of damaged streets. In extremely hot weather, both asphalt and concrete roadways can often buckle, distorting the pavement to a point where a passing vehicle can become severely damaged—and their drivers and any passengers can be injured. Drivers should be both cognizant to and cautious of such damage, and report any such instance to the appropriate authorities.

Finally on the point of temperatures, one should always be aware of weather conditions. Even in times of calm and uneventful weather, it is always a good policy to either keep a weather radio on an open broadcast, or monitor daily weather forecasts. In many cases, weather conditions can change very rapidly, being able to anticipate changing forecasts can allow one to adapt to changing weather conditions.

After A Drought

Depending on whether economic losses that may have occurred as a result of drought were residential, commercial, or agricultural, recovering from a moderate or prolonged drought can be a relatively quick or lengthy ordeal. For residential dwellers and commercial business-owners, water-saving practices can be cut-back in lieu of pre-drought water use once it has been determined that precipitation (and water) levels are back to normal. In most cases, local officials and/or meteorologists will make an announcement to the effect that any water-use restrictions have been lifted, and that it is safe to resume normal water use (levels).

Outdoors, the combination of precipitation, higher water-source levels, and cooler temperatures will cause the deterioration of plants and crops to slowing down—or stop altogether. But in some cases, lawns or field-crops may be beyond recovery. If a lawn has received as little as ¼th to ½ an inch (6.35 mm to 12.70 mm) of water a month, the grass "crowns" are likely still active and therefore salvageable. If a lawn has gone completely without any water, it is likely that many areas of the yard are completely dead.

In the case of dead lawns, re-landscaping may be the only option. Begin by top-dressing the lawn with a good-quality black soil or compost to provide a base where the new grass seeds (or plants) can take root and germinate (as mentioned previously, compost can aid plants in retaining moisture as well as in breaking down any dead grass). During the approximate 7 to 14 days it takes for grass to germinate, the seedlings must be kept moist, but not overly saturated. Watering practices will later need to be modified to accommodate changes as grass (and plants) begin to mature.

For farmers, post-drought actions might include filing claims if any economic losses were incurred as a result of drought. In such a case, farmers should be prepared to contact their insurance agent and begin initiating a crop loss claim, with a recommended follow up made in writing (a copy should be maintained and kept for personal records). As a standard procedure, most crop insurance companies will arrange for a loss adjuster to inspect any damaged crops. In some instances, the end of a drought may occur in a manner timely enough to avoid a total crop loss before its anticipated harvesting. If the timing allows a window of opportunity for production and/or food crops to be replanted, it is recommended that a crop should be switched to a type which doesn't require as much of a growing period (and/or labor intensity). However, it is ultimately up to the affected farmer/planter to decide whether such an option is worth consideration. In the final analysis, the choices are switching to another crop (if time permits), or contacting one's crop insurance agent for a loss assessment.

What to Avoid

Just as there is a level of near-inevitability for any natural (or manmade) disaster, precautions and planning can limit the possibility of both injury and/or death to those individuals such events might affect. The failure to plan and simple ignorance of the consequences are sure-fire ways to increase the likelihood of potential harm during extremely hot weather events. Additionally, bad decisions will invariably lead to counter-productive actions. Among the actions that one should avoid prior to, and during a extremely hot temperatures are:

- Not planning ahead. In most things that matter, preparation is always better than chance. Stocking up on supplies, preparing the interiors of homes and other dwellings for hot weather, and having access to information such as weather reports can save a life during extreme hot weather events.

- Failure to dress appropriately for the weather. Indoors at home, it is fine to wear as little clothing as possible (when appropriate). When you are at home wear as little clothing as possible to help keep cool. Outdoors, lightweight, light-colored, loose fitting (but comfortable) clothing should be worn. Such garments should that cover as much of the skin as possible should be worn to protect against over-exposure to the sun's intense rays. Clothing made up of natural fibers such as cotton, linen, and silk are better at absorbing sweat—which allows the skin to breathe (synthetic fabrics such as some polyesters tend to stick to the skin during heavy perspiration). A well-vented, wide-brimmed type hat should be worn to protect vital areas of the face (while allowing for excessive body heat to escape through the head).
- Wearing dark-colored and/or restrictive clothing on hot days. While light-colored fabrics tend to reflect both light and heat (which helps maintain normal body temperatures), dark-colored fabrics tend to absorb heat, making the body feel hotter.
- Using an electric fan in an attempt to cool down on days in which the temperature exceeds 90°F (32°C). Air such high temperatures, fans will just re-circulate hot air—making the body feel warmer.
- Maintaining the normal use of power levels during extremely hot weather. Heat waves and hot weather tend to trigger an increased demand in the use of electrical power as people attempt to stay cool. All unnecessary power use should be curtailed during these peak use periods.
- Leaving children and pets in a locked car on hot days. Studies show that an enclosed vehicle can begin producing temperatures that lethal to both people and animals in less than 30 minutes.
- Constantly re-hydrating by drinking water (or other non-alcoholic beverages). During extremely hot weather, human bodies can dehydrate rapidly—at times, even before symptoms of either thirst or dehydration begin showing up. Our bodies perspire at an increased rate in an effort to keep us cool during hot weather. The constant loss of bodily fluids during this process necessitates the need to keep cool drinking water nearby in order to prevent heat-related illnesses.
- Wasting water unnecessarily during droughts. Water is such a precious commodity that many areas will initiate water restrictions during periods of low precipitation, low water-source levels. Individuals can help conserve communal (shared) water supplies by curtailing their water use during such times. Taking shorter showers, water lawns/crops less, and curtailing recreational activities that involve the use of water are just a few of the steps one can take to preserve limited water availability.
- Not considering alternative methods of irrigating plants and/or crops. Research the many options available to maximize the use of limited water outside of traditional watering and irrigation methods. These endeavors will allow for the continual hydration of plants and crops, while taking into account the lower availability of water supplies.

Summary

Many of the same reasons that make heat waves a danger also apply to droughts. However, there are two major differences that give droughts their own distinct type of inherent dangers. The first of these differences is that droughts can last anywhere from several weeks to several years. Because of the slow onset of droughts, their cost is often only estimated. As droughts become more frequent and intense, unprepared areas of the world can suffer catastrophic water shortages, leading to destroyed crops and even starvation. Serious drought conditions in underdeveloped regions can even lead to increased chances for major disease outbreaks.

Something else to consider—even if water shortages aren't catastrophic during a drought, these shortages nonetheless tend to put a strain on community water management efforts. When there is a drought, there is less water available for growing crops, farming animals, industry, and our private/personal use. Droughts also impact the environment by causing soil erosion, potential harm to animals, an increase in food prices, and a reduction our basic water supplies. Droughts are hard to predict and also hard to live with. When a drought continues for a long time, entire towns can be at risk for running out of water. As an example, many areas in Australia have water restrictions to help save water, while other areas use a combination of water recycling, desalination plants and newly-dug wells in order to secure more water for their residents.

Insomuch as heat waves are concerned, extremely hot temperatures are every bit the danger that more spectacular events such as hurricanes, tornadoes, and floods are. In fact, heat kills more people worldwide than most other weather events combined. Much of the reason for the high death-rate during extreme heat is because many of the dangers under such conditions are underestimated. The onsets of heat-related illnesses are often ignored—until it is too late. Lapses in planning, judgment, and bad decisions are—in most cases—at the root of most casualties.

Droughts can (and do) occur in many areas of the world that undergo seasonal changes. These areas include North America. In the United States, both droughts and heat waves occur in every state. This means that at some point, almost every American will go through one at some point. And preparing for the inevitable is the best was to avoid experiencing the worst potential effects of these extreme weather events.

The No-Nonsense Guide To Heat Wave, Drought, & Hot Weather Safety

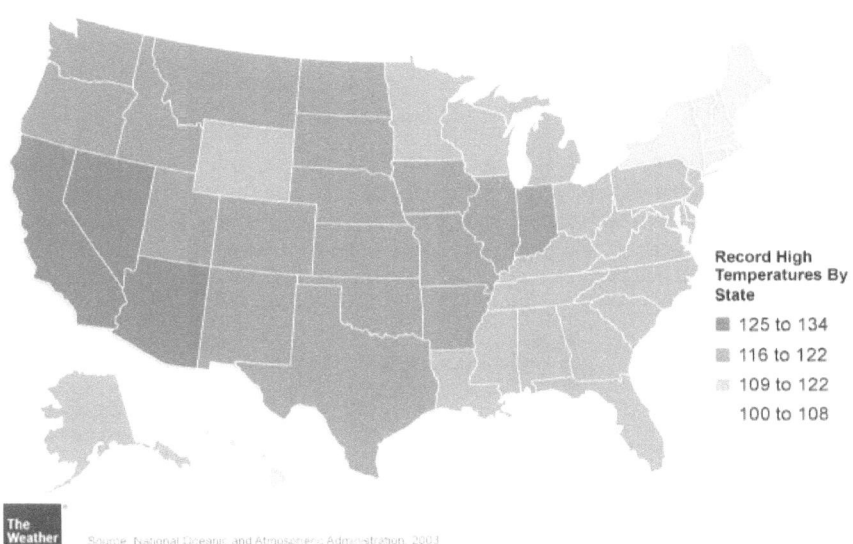

**Record High
Temperatures By
State**

- 125 to 134
- 116 to 122
- 109 to 122
- 100 to 108

The
Weather
Channel

Source: National Oceanic and Atmospheric Administration, 2001
ITS Mapping and Analysis Center Washington, DC

Notes

Heat Wave & Drought History

The following extreme heat-related events are notable for the resulting losses in human lives, as well as in property losses and overall economic impact of affected regions. Some of these events have produced extreme weather records that still stand to this day. These heat-related events provide an illustration of the varying impact (and effects) these extreme heat events have.

Date	Location	Impact/Significance
The "Great Famine" (Drought) 1876-1879	From (several provinces of) Northern China, to parts of Southern Russia, and as far as Eastern Iran.	Also known as "the Great Famine." this drought cut a large swath through parts of Asia over a period of nearly 4 years. As entire rivers dried up, an estimated 6 to 9 million people perished from the resulting lack of food and water.
The Marble Bar Heat Wave (1923-24)	Bar Marble, north-western portion of the province of Western Australia	The Bar Marble Heat Wave continues to hold the record for the world's longest and most intense (temperature-wise) heat wave. From October 31, 1923 to April 7 the following year, the temperature at Bar Marble, Western Australia reached or exceeded 100°F (or 38°C) a total of 160 days. The highest temperature recorded during the record spell was 116°F (47°C) on January 18, 1924.
The "Dust Bowl" Era (1930-1936)	Central United States, entailing the states of Oklahoma, Nebraska, Texas Kansas, Colorado, and New Mexico.	This period of time, also known as the "Dirty Thirties," and the "Dust Bowl Days," this period was the most destructive drought in U.S. history. This prolonged period of dry weather, along with poor soil management practices (including overuse) lead to unprecedented levels of soil erosion and crop losses. The result was that the soil in extensive regions of land in the American Great Plains quite literally turned to dust. Heavy winds would often pick up and whip this dust into enormous dust storms dubbed "black rollers" or "black blizzards."
The 1981-1984 African Drought &	Regions of Eastern Africa,	During this crisis, over a dozen

Famine	particularly the country of Ethiopia	nations of Africa were under severe drought. As lakes and waterbeds completely dried up, an estimated 20,000 people a month starved to death in the famine that resulted (aided by ongoing wars in some affected regions). Although the exact death toll is not completely known, it is estimated that over 1 million people in all died as a direct result of the drought.
The Drought of 1988 -89	Sections of the West, the central Mid- and Upper Midwest U.S. and into parts of Southern Canada.	At its peak, the Drought of 1988-90 affected over a third of the continental U.S., and was costliest drought in the country's history (with damage cost estimates ranging from $35 billion to in excess of $60 billion). Making the effects of the drought worse were the numerous forest fires that occurred due to dry conditions. In 1988, 793,880 acres of Yellowstone National Park burned, prompting the first complete closure of the park in history. The record drought also produced a series of heat waves that resulted in between 4,000 and 15,000 by some estimates.
The Chicago Heat Wave (1995)	The Midwestern United States, including the city of Chicago	In July of 1995, the Midwestern region of the U.S. experienced several days of triple-digit temperatures, along with dangerously high humidity levels. This event caught many social and governmental agencies responsible for social responses off-guard. Social forces combined with an ineffective response to make this an unusually deadly heat wave. Many victims were elderly and lived alone, often in neglected neighborhoods with high crime…and with no one to provide well-being checks on these individuals. The city's inability to commit resources to the event, along with the lack of resources of those affects converged to result in between 500-750 deaths in the city alone, with several more in other nearby major cities.
The Millennium Drough: (1995-	Most of continental Australia	The 1995-2009 in Australia, also

2009)		known as the "Millennium Drought" was caused by a prolonged string of consistently high temperatures, limited rainfall, and a change in local and regional weather patterns caused by the mid-ocean phenomenon known as "El Nino." This resulted in the wholesale drying up of rivers and lakes, massive crop losses, and a severe reduction in available water resources for much of the country. The latter effect led to a water supply crisis that forced the government to build—for the first time—to build desalination (that filtered surrounding ocean waters for available use).
The 2003 European Heat Wave	Central and Southern Europe	In mid-2003, a record-breaking heat wave swept across Europe. In many affected countries, the temperatures reached triple-digits for more than 2 weeks. Because many homes in most of the affected countries didn't contain air conditioners, the death toll was exceedingly high and widespread. France fared the worst with an estimated death toll of 14,000 people, mostly among the poor and elderly. Forest fires plagued Portugal. Melting glaciers caused flash floods in Switzerland. Crops failed in Southern Europe. All told, between 20,000 and 35,000 people died

The No-Nonsense Guide To Heat Wave, Drought, & Hot Weather Safety

Glossary of Hot Weather-Related Terms

Drought – is said to occur when abnormally dry weather settles over a particular region for a prolonged period of time. This extended period of time is usually of a sufficient duration as to cause water deficiencies (in the form of low precipitation and/or low water-source levels) in the affected area. These deficiencies can cause such problems as crop damage and a general water-supply shortage. The general definition for what constitute a "drought" can vary, depending on location. In Australia, a drought is defined as the prolonged absence or marked deficiency of precipitation (rain).

Dust Bowl – was the widely-used designation of a region located in the central portion of the continental U.S. during the 1930's. The "Dust Bowl" label was a reflection of the physical (and visible) effects of an extreme drought that had occurred during that economically tumultuous time period. For the better part of the decade, large swaths of land encompassing parts of southern Nebraska, Oklahoma, Kansas, and northern Texas experienced an absence of vegetation due to a combination of extreme drought, over farming, and soil erosion. These factors created a unique set of conditions that resulted in the soil being replaced by dry dust that made farming in the region all but impossible. As the physical geography of the land had come to resemble the geographic features of a desert rather than a soil-rich plain, the region took on the infamous title of a "Dust Bowl." During this period, the lad had become so dry and conditions so extreme that region was frequented by intense sandstorms caused by winds carrying the dry dust for miles. These dust storms were called "black blizzards" by residents at the time.

El Niño – is the name given to the periodically-occurring ocean-based phenomenon that alters weather pattern globally, resulting in deviations from normally occurring weather patterns. This phenomenon involves a major warming of the equatorial waters the eastern Pacific Ocean that occurs between every 3 to 7 years. This ocean-warming patterns was designated "El Niño" because of the time of year it tends to take shape (El Niño is Spanish for the "Christ Child" because it often begins around Christmas).

Heat index –is a meteorological-based quantification of how the combination of heat (i.e., air temperatures) and humidity actually feels to the human body. The result is an "apparent temperature" that is supposed to accurately symbolize how the weather "feels."

Heat wave – is a period of abnormally hot weather (characterized by high temperatures and humidity levels) lasting anywhere from several days to several weeks.

High Pressure (see: Pressure)

Humidity – relates to the measurable amount of water vapor in the atmosphere. In terms of general forecasting, the two (of three) main measurements of humidity are *absolute humidity* (the actual measure of water content of air), and *relative humidity* (see also, "relative humidity"), expressed as a percent, measures the current absolute humidity relative to the maximum for that temperature. Just as with other meteorological measurements, both the definitions and the thresholds for recognizing conditions such as humidity vary from region to region. In Canada, humidity is described as "the amount of moisture in the air."

Jet streams – are the intensely strong corridor of winds concentrated within narrow bands in the upper atmosphere along certain latitudes circling the globe. The jet stream(s) often "steers" surface weather patterns such as front and low pressure systems. In other instances, storms and organized systems tend to travel along jet streams across entire regions.

La Niña – the opposite of El Niño, La Niña is an ocean-based weather phenomenon characterized by a cooling of the equatorial waters in the Pacific Ocean. Like El Niño, the La Niña event tends to affect weather patterns globally when they occur.

Pressure – is the force exerted by the interaction of the atmosphere and gravity. Also known as "atmospheric pressure," this meteorological occurrence tends to help shape weather patterns as well as storms.

Radiation – is the energy emitted in the form of electromagnetic waves. Radiation has differing characteristics depending upon the wavelength from one of the electromagnetic spectrum to the other. Radiation from the Sun has a short wavelength (ultraviolet) while energy re-radiated from the Earth's surface and the atmosphere has a long wavelength (infrared). Short wavelength radiation is the type that is partially responsible for the occurrence of sunburn incidents.

Relative humidity - The amount of water vapor in the air, compared to the amount the air could hold if it was totally saturated. It is expressed and measured as a percentage. The percent of "relative humidity" in the air is usually broadcast as part of daily weather segments during weather reports (mostly in the developed regions of the world).

Temperate Zone - the part of the earth's surface lying between the tropic of Cancer and the Arctic Circle (specific latitudes) in the Northern Hemisphere or between the tropic of Capricorn and the Antarctic Circle in the Southern Hemisphere, and characterized by having a climate that is warm in the summer, cold in the winter, and moderate in the spring and fall. Temperate zones are where the majority of the world's seasonal changes take place.

UV Index - The ultraviolet index or "UV Index" is an international standard measurement of the strength of ultraviolet (UV) radiation (see "ultraviolet radiation") from the sun at a particular point in time, as it affects a particular region.

Ultraviolet Radiation - Ultraviolet Radiation (UV) is simply one form of energy comprising the electromagnetic radiation spectrum emitted by the sun.

Appendix A:

Ultraviolet Radiation & Sun-Exposure Explained

Visible Light/UV

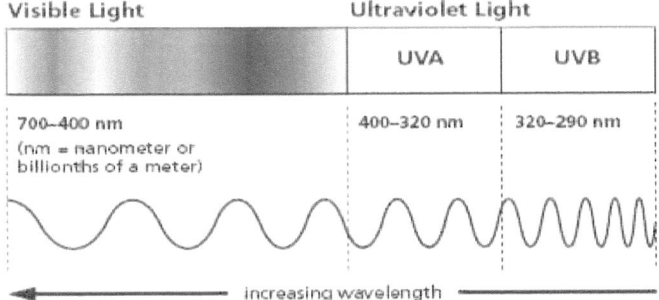

Simply put, ultraviolet radiation (also known as UV radiation or ultraviolet rays) is a form of energy that "radiates" from the sun (and/or other stars), and travels through space to Earth (and beyond). This energy tends to manifest itself in the most common forms of heat and light. These rays, along with others, are part of a broader electromagnetic radiation spectrum. While most forms of radiation within the spectrum are visible, other types are not. Examples of the invisible portion of electromagnetic radiation are gamma rays, X-rays, visible light, infrared rays, and radio waves. The progression of electromagnetic radiation through space can be visualized in different ways. Some experiments suggest that these rays travel in the form of waves (physicist scan actually measure the length of different wave types along the spectrum, which are classified as "wavelengths")

The distinguishing factor among the different types of electromagnetic radiation wavelengths is their energy content; smaller wavelength radiation types contain more energy. Shorter wavelength ultraviolet radiation is more energetic than visible radiation. To be more specific: Ultraviolet rays have a wavelength between approximately 100 nanometers (nm) and 400 nanometers whereas visible radiation includes wavelengths between 400 and 780 nanometers.

Approximately 99% of the sun's rays are in the form of visible light, ultraviolet rays, and infrared rays (also known as heat). Man-made lamps can also emit UV radiation, and are often used for experimental purposes. Light enables us to see, and heat keeps us from being cold. However, ultraviolet rays often carry the unfortunate circumstance of containing too much energy. For example, infrared rays create heat in much the same way as rubbing your hands together does. The energy contained in the infrared rays causes the molecules of the substance it hits to vibrate back and forth.

Ultraviolet rays can be subdivided into three different wavelength bands - UV-A, UV-B, and UV-C. These classifications are based on the amount of energy they contain and their effects on biological matter. Insomuch as hot weather and summer safety, only UV-A and UV-B rays are relevant.

Despite UV-B rays' lower energy level and longer wavelengths, some of them can reach the earth's surface from the sun. UV-A radiation tends to pass through the earth's atmosphere almost unfiltered. As both UV-B and UV-A rays can be detrimental to our health, it is important that we protect ourselves. This can be done through a variety of ways. The most obvious is to reduce the amount of time one spends in the sun, particularly between the hours of 11 am and 3 pm, when the sun is at its highest in the sky. The UV Protection Chart on the following page is a way to determine what (or whether) protective precautions should be taken given the UV Index.

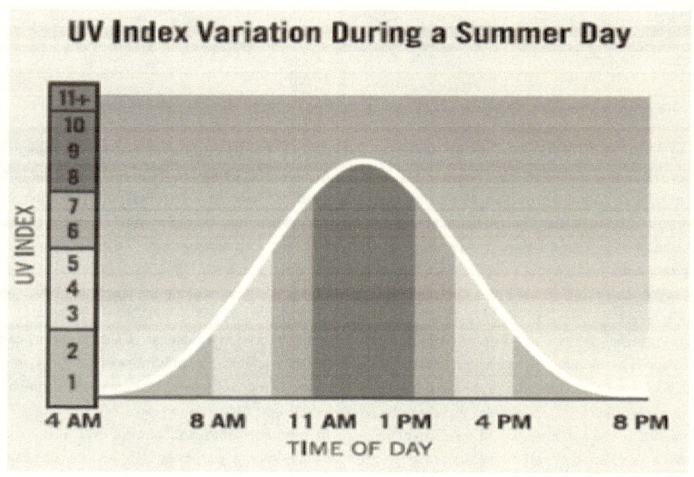

The No-Nonsense Guide To Heat Wave, Drought, & Hot Weather Safety

Appendix B
Degrees of Sunburn

Sunburn is a heat-related issue that occurs in varying degrees of severity, based on unprotected exposure to the sun's ultraviolent rays. This is to say that the longer the exposure to sunlight, the more extensive the potential damage to skin tissue that results. In general, most people experience *some* level of sunburn during their lives.

First degree
The differences between sunburn degrees have to do with the depth and the extent of a particular burn. If the surface of the skin (the top layer) only is affected by over-exposure to the sun's rays, it is considered a "first-degree sunburn." First-degree sunburns are characterized by skin that is red, mildly irritated, and dry. These types of sunburns don't normally blister (Blistering indicates the burn was deep enough to injure the second layer of skin). In many cases, the soreness and skin discoloration associated with this mildest type of sunburn may not show up for several hours after sun exposure. The changes in the color and condition of this level of skin damage are temporary, and usually disappear in a few days. This is also the most common type of sunburn.

Second degree

The second type of sunburn/skin damage is known as "second-degree sunburn." Second-degree sunburn is far more harmful to the skin than first-degree burns—with potentially lasting damage as a result. This type of sunburn causes damage which can appear soon after exposure to the sun and is recognized by one or more of the following:

- Extremely red appearance to the skin

- Prominent heat felt from the skin's surface

- Severe pain to the skin even when it is not touched

- Blistering which may weep serous fluid (blistering is a sign that deeper skin layers are starting to be affected)
- Swelling to the affected area of the body.

This type of sunburn can cause swelling and blistering, which is an indication that deep skin layers and nerve endings have been damaged. With second-degree sunburns, there may be an increase in the surface temperature of the affected areas of skin (i.e., the affected areas of skin may actually begin radiating heat) from the skin), with some leaking of fluids from the affected areas. Second-degree sunburns are very painful, with severe cases producing fever, vomiting, dehydration and secondary infection in some individuals. And like first-degree sunburns, the changes in the appearance and condition of the skin will usually fade after about a week (longer than in the case of first-degree sunburns). However, the damaging effects can last longer, as greater and repeated deep skin damage from the sun's UV rays can increase the likelihood for several types of skin cancers.

Third degree
Although very rare, there have been instances where individuals have experienced what could be considered "third-degree sunburn." This can be described as a continued exposure to the sun's damaging UV rays despite the presence of (a) major second-degree sunburn. In this most extreme and rarest of cases, the skin is completely

burned. The skin may appear very dark-red or even darker in color, with lower levels of the skin blistering and oozing fluids. The affected person is agony, even when the skin hasn't been touched. The person may experience many or all of the more severe symptoms as those of (a) major second-degree sunburn. At this point, it is imperative to seek professional help in the form of an Emergency Medical Technician (EMT) or an emergency room physician.

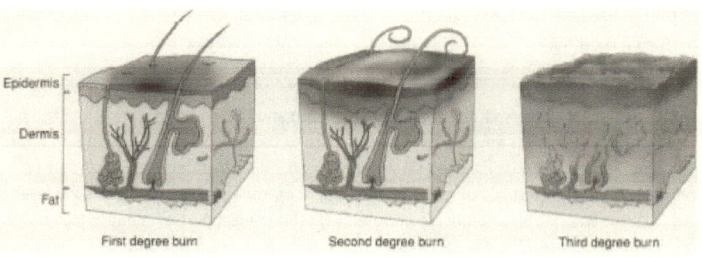

Appendix C
Drought(s) & Drought-Related Disasters by Countries

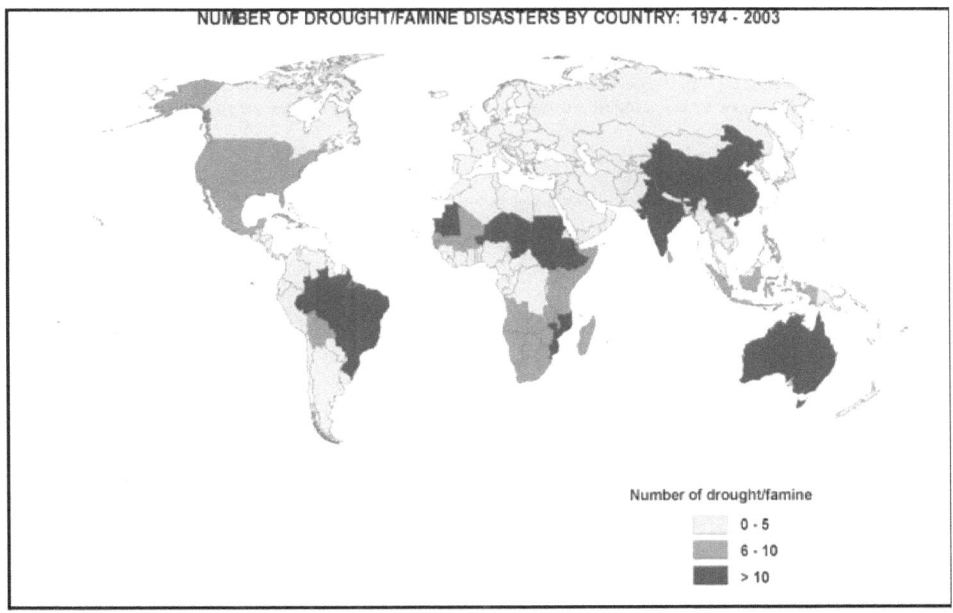

The No-Nonsense Guide To Heat Wave, Drought, & Hot Weather Safety

Appendix D
Federal Emergency Management Agency (FEMA) contact information by region

As an extensive government agency, FEMA administrative resources (as well as contact information) have been somewhat decentralized. This is to say that, in order to expedite any assistance to local and state governments (and to limit the potential for bureaucratic confusion), FEMA was divided into regional offices that oversee regional "zones." These *Regional Operations*

Offices serve as the arms of the central agency's headquarters (located in Washington D.C.) and through which all policy, managerial, resource and administrative actions effecting coordination between headquarters are initiated.

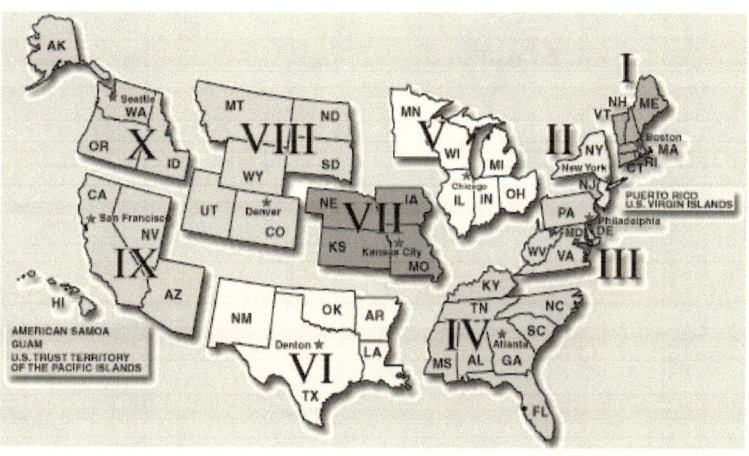

Region	Location	States Serving
Region I	Boston, MA	CT, MA, ME, NH, RI, VT
Region II	New York, NY	NJ, NY, PR, USVI
Region III	Philadelphia, PA	DC, DE, MD, PA, VA, WV
Region IV	Atlanta, GA	AL, FL, GA, KY, MS, NC, SC, TN
Region V	Chicago, IL	IL, IN, MI, MN, OH, WI

The No-Nonsense Guide To Heat Wave, Drought, & Hot Weather Safety

Region	Location	States Serving
Region VI	Denton, TX	AR, LA, NM, OK, TX
Region VII	Kansas City, MO	IA, KS, MO, NE
Region VIII	Denver, CO	CO, MT, ND, SD, UT, WY
Region IX	Oakland, CA	AZ, CA, HI, NV, GU, AS, CNMI, RMI, FM
Region X	Bothell, WA	AK, ID, OR, WA

Contact:

FEMA Region I
99 High St.
Boston, MA 02110
1-877-336-2734
Email

Federal Region II
26 Federal Plaza
New York, NY 10278-0002
Telephone: (212) 680-3600
FEMA-R2-ExternalAffairs@fema.dhs.gov

Puerto Rico and Virgin Islands

Mailing address:
Carribean Division
PO Box 70105
San Juan PR 00936-0105

Physical address:
New San Juan Office Bldg
159 Calle Chardon, 6th Floor
Hato Rey, PR 00918
Telephone: (787) 296-3500

FEMA Region III
One Independence Mall, 6th Floor
615 Chestnut Street
Philadelphia, PA 19106-4404
(215) 931-5500

FEMA Region IV

Federal Emergency Management Agency
3003 Chamblee Tucker Road
Atlanta, GA 30341
Office: 770-220-5200
Fax Number: 770-220-5230

FEMA Region V
Federal Emergency Management Agency
536 South Clark Street, 6th Floor
Chicago, IL 60605
(312) 408-5500

FEMA Region VI
Federal Emergency Management Agency
FRC 800 North Loop 288
Denton, TX 76209-3698
E-Mail: FEMA-R6-RRCC-PrivateSector@fema.dhs.gov
Tribal Affairs
E-Mail Norma.Reyes@fema.dhs.gov
Telephone: 940-898-5233

FEMA Region VII or Federal Emergency Management Agency
9221 Ward Parkway, Suite 300
Kansas City, MO. 64114-3372
Telephone: (816) 283-7061
Tribal Contact
E-mail: jonathan.weinberg@fema.dhs.gov
Telephone: (816) 809-4128

FEMA Region VIII or Federal Emergency Management Agency
Federal Emergency Management Agency
Denver Federal Center
Building 710, Box 25267
Denver, CO 80225-0267
(303) 235-4800

FEMA Region IX
1111 Broadway, Oakland, CA 94607
Phone:(510) 627-7140
Pacific Area Office
(808) 851-7900
Southern California Field Office
(626) 431-3000

FEMA Region X or Federal Emergency Management Agency
Federal Regional Center
130 - 228th Street, Southwest
Bothell, WA 98021-8627
(425) 487-4600

Appendix D:
Useful Smart Phones & Computer App (Applications)

1.   Weather Bug (Free)

An all-around weather app for both phones and computers (Weather Bug Desktop), Weather Bug provides real-time weather forecasts for the users' vicinity for a 10-day period. In addition, this app contains a real-time sensor that warns of dangerous lightning threats for the users' area. Created and sponsored by Earth Networks.

2.   The Weather Channel (Free)

Also available for desktop/laptop computers, this application—like Weather Bug—provides an active 10-day weather forecast for the user vicinity. In addition, the issues real-time severe weather bulletins such as those issued for heat watches and heat warnings.

Many other similar applications of various costs can be found by searching various online application sources such as Google Play and the Apple-supported i-Tunes .

Index

The No-Nonsense Guide To Heat Wave, Drought, & Hot Weather Safety

References

"About Drought." American Red Cross website. Accessed 3 March 2014

"California's 100-year drought" September 3, 2014 Doyle Rice, USA TODAY

Cohen, J. "Heat Waves Throughout History." 2 5 June 2013. History Channel website. Accessed 29 July 2014.

Deardorff, J. "How Extreme Heat Attacks the Body." Chicago Tribune website. 20 July 2011. Accessed 15 July 2014

"Disaster Assistance Program." The United States Department of Agriculture website. 26 September 2014. Accessed 15 October 2014

"Drought." Ready.gov website. 13 November 2013 Accessed 3 March 2014.

"Drought and Extreme Heat." Stearns County, Minnesota goverment website. Accessed 3 March 2014

"Drought Basics." National Drought Mitigation Center website. 20 February 2014

"Drought." U.S. Government Disaster Assistance website. 08 October 2014 Accessed 15 October 2014

"Extreme Heat: A Prevention Guide to Promote Your Personal Health and Safety." Centers for Disease Control and Prevention (CDC) website. 31 July 2009. Accessed 31 May 2014

"Extreme Weather - Heat." Washington D.C. Homeland Security and Emergency Management Agency website. Accessed 6 April 2014.

"How To File a Crop Insurance Claim." United States Department of Agriculture Risk Management Agency GPO August 2008. Print.

"French heat toll almost 15,000." BBC News. 25 September 2003.

Glazer M.D., J L. "Management of Heatstroke and Heat Exhaustion." American Family Physician June 01, 2005. Print

"Global Solar UV Index: A Practical Guide". World Health Organization. 2002. Print.

"Growing Toward More Efficient Water Use: Linking Development Infrastructures, and Drinking Water Policies." United States Environmental Protection Agency. January 2006. Accessed 31 July 2014

Grubenhoff J, du Ford K, Roosevelt G. Heat-Related Illness. Clinical Pediatric Emergency Medicine. 2007; 8(1):59-64. Print

Epstein M.D., J. H., Wang M.D., S. Q. "Understanding UVA and UVB," Skin Cancer.org website. 2014 Accessed 7 July 2014.

"Extreme Heat." Ready.gov website. 29 Jan 2014. Accessed 7 July 2014

Hayes, M.J., Brian D. Wardlow, Mark D. Svoboda, Tsegaye Tadesse, and Kelly H. Smith. 2009. "Sharpening the Focus on Drought — New Monitoring and Assessment Tools at the National Drought Mitigation Center." Earthzine. March 30.

"Heat: A Major Killer." National Weather Service website. Updated 28 July 2014 Accessed 30 July 2014

"Heat Cramps." Web MD website 30 Oct 2013. Accessed 8 July 2014.

"Heat: During the Heat Wave." The Weather Channel website. Accessed 8 July 2014

"Heat Exhaustion." University of Maryland School of Medicine website. 7 May 2013 Accessed 7 July 2014.

"Heat Index." National Weather Service website. 21 October 2011. Accessed 16 July 2014.

"Heat-Related Illnesses - Prevention." WebMD website. 30 Aug 2013. Accessed 7 July 2014.

"Heat Stress." OSHA Technical Manual (OTM). OSHA Directive TED 01-00-015 [TED 1-0.15A], (1999, January 20). Print.

"Heat Wave Safety." American Red Cross website. Accessed 8 July 2014

Hu L.W. et al (2010), Diurnal Variations in Solar Ultraviolet Radiation on Horizontal and Vertical Plane. Iranian Journal of Public Health, 39(3): 70–81. Print.

"Keep Your Cool in Hot Weather." Centers for Disease Control and Prevention (CDC) Website 30 June 2014. Accessed 15 July 2014

Knutson, C. L. 2008. "The role of water conservation in drought planning." Journal of Soil and Water Conservation 63(5). Accessed 30 July 2014

The No-Nonsense Guide To Heat Wave, Drought, & Hot Weather Safety

Krakowski AC, Kaplan _A. Exposure to radiation from the sun. In: Auerbach PS, ed. Wilderness Medicine. 6th ed. Philadelphia, Fa: 2011:chap. 14.

Lim HW, Hawk JLM. Photodermatologic disorders. In: Bolognia JL, Jorizzo JL, Schaffer JV, eds. Dermatology . 3rd ed. Philadelphia, Pa: Elsevier Saunders; 2012:chap 87.

"Monitoring Drought." NOAA – Climate Services Portal 15 November 2013 Accessed 21 February 2014

"Occupational Heat Exposure." Occupational Safety & Health Administration (OSHA) website. Accessed 8 August 2014

Pulwarty, R., D. Wilhite, D. Diodato, and D. Nelson, 2007. "Drought in changing environments — Creating a Roadmap, Vehicles and Drivers." Natural Hazards Observer. May 07. Accessed 30 July 2014

Sanders, S. "California Rolls Out Statewide Restrictions On Water Use." National Public Radio. 15 Jul 2014.

Sanders, Sam "California Rolls Out Statewide Restrictions On Water Use" National Public Radio July 15, 2014

Sobell, Jeffrey M. "What Happens When You Get a Sunburn?" Scientific American website. 6 Aug 2011 Accessed 16 July 2014

SOSE Alive 3, pp. 178–9 ? SOSE Alive Geography 2, pp. 136–7 2004 Accessed 3 March 2014

Stöppler, M.D., M C. "11 Tips for Surviving A Heat Wave Without Air-Conditioning." MedicineNet website. 20 Jume 2012. Accessed 7 July 2013

"The Basics of Crop Insurance." Pro Ag website. Accessed 4 March 2014

Wilhite, D.A. 2006. "Drought Monitoring and Early Warning: Concepts, Progress and Future Challenges." Geneva: World Meteorological Organization. WMO No. 1006.

"Understanding Humidity." USAToday website 2011. Accessed 16 July 2014.
http://usatoday30.usatoday.com/weather/whumdef.htm

"U.S. Drought Monitor Background." U.S. Drought Monitor website. 2014. 20 February 2014.
http://droughtmonitcr.unl.edu/

The No-Nonsense Guide To Heat Wave, Drought, & Hot Weather Safety

The No-Nonsense Guide To Heat Wave, Drought, & Hot Weather Safety

The No-Nonsense Guide To Heat Wave, Drought, & Hot Weather Safety

Page 14:
The Weather Channel website

Page 15:
WebMd.com

Page 17:
http://chughtailab.com/

Page 23:
NOLA.com website

Page 24:
The Atlantic.com
http://www.theatlantic.com/infocus/2011/09/more-texas-wildfires/100141/

Page 28:
Earth Online Media.com

Page 32:
http://www.ehow.com/list_7532252_warning-signs-drought.html

Page 54:
http://www.scrd.ca/sprinkling-regulations

Page 45:
National Oceanic and Atmospheric Adminstration website

Page 52:
Gardeners research.com

Page 64:
Appendix A:
http://www.skincancer.org

Page 65:
Appendix A:
http://livelovelashdenver.com

Page 65:
Appendix A:
gbhealthwatch.com

The No-Nonsense Guide To Heat Wave, Drought, & Hot Weather Safety

The No-Nonsense Guide To Heat Wave, Drought, & Hot Weather Safety

Other Books in the No-Nonsense Safety Guide Series Published By Lulu Books & Beyond the Spectrum

The No-Nonsense Guide To Tornado Safety

• Paperback: 84 pages • Publisher: lulu.com (November 22, 2013) • Language: English • ISBN-10: 1304648648 • ISBN-13: 978-1304648648 • Product Dimensions: 9 x 6 x 0.2 inches • Shipping Weight: 6.4 ounce

The No-Nonsense Guide To Blizzard Safety

• Paperback: 54 pages • Publisher: lulu.com (December 21, 2013) • Language: English • ISBN-10: 9781304709394 • Product Dimensions: 9 x 6 x 0.2 inches • Shipping Weight: 0.28 pounds

The No-Nonsense Guide To Flood Safety.

The No-Nonsense Guide To Heat Wave, Drought, & Hot Weather Safety

• Paperback: 60 pages • Publisher: lulu.com (November 22, 2013) • Language: English • ISBN-10: 1304648613 • Product Dimensions: 9 x 6 x 0.2 inches

The No-Nonsense Guide To Hurricane Safety.

• Paperback: 59 pages • Publisher: lulu.com (December 20, 2013) • Language: English • ISBN-10: 9781304733030 • Product Dimensions: 9 x 6 x 0.2 inches

The No-Nonsense Guide To Earthquake Safety.

• Paperback: 104 pages • Publisher: lulu.com (June 11, 2014) • Language: English • ISBN-10: 9781312274105 • Product Dimensions: 9 x 6 x 0.2 inches

Other upcoming books in the series include: "The No-Nonsense Guide to Fire Safety," and "The No-Nonsense Guide To Automobile Safety."

The No-Nonsense Guide To Heat Wave, Drought, & Hot Weather Safety